THE TASTE OF
SEAFOOD

THE TASTE OF
SEAFOOD

Antonio Piccinardi

Webb & Bower
MICHAEL JOSEPH

First published in Great Britain 1988 by
Webb & Bower (Publishers) Limited
9 Colleton Crescent, Exeter, Devon EX2 4BY
in association with Michael Joseph Limited
27 Wright's Lane, London W8 5TZ

Photographs: Emilio Fabio Simion
Drawings of fish, molluscs, crustaceans: Ezio Giglioli
Drawings pp. 186–9: Margrit Hofmann

The author would like to thank Laura Raffo and Cinzia
Wybranowski for their kind assistance.

Translated from the Italian by Elaine Hardy
Copyright © 1985 Arnoldo Mondadori Editore
S.p.A., Milan
Copyright © 1986 Arnoldo Mondadori Editore
S.p.A., Milan for the English translation

British Library Cataloguing in Publication Data
Piccinardi, Antonio
    The taste of seafood.
    1. Food. Seafood dishes—Recipes
    I. Title.   II. Piatti di mare. *English*
    641.6′9

ISBN 0-86350-244-X

Printed and bound in Italy by Arnoldo Mondadori Editore,
Verona.

Contents

The secrets of the sea

The saying 'cooking is an art' is never more true than where fish is concerned. Fish must not only be fresh and well cooked; it must also be attractively presented, recalling the culinary delights of holidays by the sea. There is certainly no sorrier sight than a solitary fish on a plate and some, such as the carp or eel, seem poor man's fare indeed unless adorned by a rich sauce. *Carp Polish style* and *Eel pie* transform both of these humbler fish into a dish fit for any table.

Of the more exotic fish, molluscs, and crustaceans, recipes are included for sea bass, turbot, sturgeon, crayfish, lobster, crab, and oysters. The very names of some dishes—*Waterzooi, Tempura, Jansson's temptation*—suggest delights unknown.

Among the other secrets to success contained in this book are suggestions as to which wines marry best with each particular dish, including selections from California, South Africa, Australia, and New Zealand as well as the more familiar European wines.

For each dish a complete menu is suggested, including a starter, main course, and dessert, offering the perfect combination of ingredients in terms of flavour and texture. The starters and main courses are all taken from, and variously combined in, the 105 recipes illustrated, each dish appearing different in each new combination.

The dessert recipes, in a separate section at the end of the book, include such tempting delights as *Wild strawberries and ice cream, Rhubarb soufflé, Calvados sorbet, Ladies' kisses, Passion fruit sorbet*, to name but a few.

Finally, there is the practical section on basic recipes, utensils, and techniques of preparation, cooking and storing fish—an essential feature in any serious cookbook. The basic recipes include many of the classic sauces, while notes are provided on the various methods of cooking fish and on the necessary equipment. Instructions on cleaning fish are accompanied by drawings clearly illustrating each step—all you need to know to turn the simplest fish dish into the finest offering.

Note on quantities

Recipes, other than those in the 'One-course dishes'
section, are intended for four people within an Italian-style
multi-course meal. Quantities may therefore be slightly
less than those found in other recipe books. 'One-course
dishes', while still for four people, are more substantial
and can be eaten either as a complete meal or as one
course among several.

Silverware, cutlery, china, saucepans and table linen for
the photographs kindly loaned by: Aris, Cantinarredo,
Christofle, Cristallo di Censo, Faenze di Faenza,
D. Farmache, Frette, Laboratorio Pesaro, Medagliani,
B. Morone, Pomellato, Porcellana bianca, L. Ricciarini,
Richard-Ginori, G. Rovere, Sebring, Vavassori.
Fish, molluscs and crustaceans provided by Pesclaudio.

One-course dishes

Seafood salad

Preparation: 1 hour
(+ 1 hour for
cleaning mussels and
razor clams)

6 baby octopus,
squid, or cuttlefish,
cleaned (total weight
350 g/12 oz)

salt and pepper
1 stick celery
225 g/8 oz mussels
275 g/10 oz razor clams
1 clove garlic
275 g/10 oz jumbo prawns
1 bunch parsley
6 tbsp oil
½ lemon

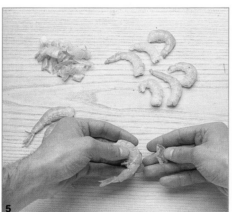

1   Gently lower the baby octopus, tentacles first, into boiling salted water. Add the chopped celery and cook for 8 minutes, then drain.

2   Wash the mussels and razor clams and leave under running water for 1 hour. Drain, place in a saucepan and sprinkle with the chopped garlic. Cover and cook gently for 4 minutes until the shells open. Remove meat from the shells and place in a dish.

3   When the octopus have cooled, cut off the tentacles and slice the bodies into rings. Place both in the dish with the mussels and razor clams.

4   Place the prawns, heads removed, in a small saucepan with a little water and salt. Cover and cook for 4 minutes.

5   Peel the prawns and add to the other seafood.

6   Rinse and dry the parsley. Chop finely and sprinkle over the mixed seafood. Season with oil, lemon juice, salt, and pepper. Stir well before serving.

Suggested menu

Seafood salad
Eel pie
Calvados sorbet

Suggested wines

Tocai del Collio, Verdicchio dei Castelli di Jesi (Italy); Chablis (France); Californian Pinot Blanc (U.S.A.); Chenin Blanc (South Africa).

Waterzooi

(Belgian eel and freshwater fish soup)

Preparation: 1¼ hours

450 g/1 lb eel
50 g/2 oz butter
1 onion
salt and pepper
mace

2 bay leaves
2 cloves
1 tsp grated lemon rind
4–5 pieces celery
a few sprigs parsley
2 225-g/8-oz trout
2 225-g/8-oz perch

Suggested menu

Waterzooi
Grilled or barbecued turbot
Floating islands

Suggested wines

Spumante Champenois dell'Oltrepò Pavese,
Tocai del Collio (Italy); Gewürztraminer
d'Alsace (France); Californian Gewürztraminer
(U.S.A.); Rhine Riesling (South Africa).

1 Clean and skin the eel and chop into 4-cm/1½-inch pieces.

2 Melt the butter in a large saucepan and brown the eel together with the finely chopped onion for 5 minutes.

3 Add 1.5 litres/2½ pints water, cover, and simmer for 15 minutes.

4 Add the salt, pepper, mace, bay leaves, cloves, grated lemon rind, celery and parsley. Cover and cook for 20 minutes until the eel is tender.

5 Pour the eel and stock through a strainer with a fine mesh, pressing to extract as much liquid as possible.

6 Clean and fillet the trout and perch.

7 Place the fillets in a large pan with the strained stock and simmer for about 10 minutes. Add salt.

8 Butter slices of bread, cut into strips, and serve with the fish soup.

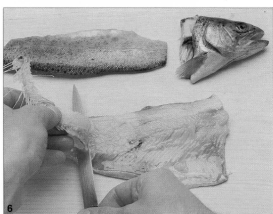

Tempura
(Japanese mixed fry)

Preparation: 2 hours

1 small spiny lobster
16 jumbo prawns
1 sole
salt and pepper
6 tbsp soy sauce
6 tbsp saké
2 tsp sugar
2 tbsp fresh
   horseradish
1 tsp powdered ginger
4 scallops
1 green pepper
1 carrot
225 g/8 oz green beans
2 eggs, 150 g/5 oz
   plain flour, oil

Suggested menu

Salmon mousse
Tempura
Fruit salad in gin

Suggested wines

Spumante Champenois dell'Oltrepò Pavese,
Sauvignon del Collio (Italy); Champagne
(France); Californian Johannisberg Riesling
(U.S.A.); Fumé Blanc (South Africa).

1 Remove the meat from the spiny lobster shell. Shell and clean the prawns, removing the heads.

2 Fillet the sole. Make a fumet by placing the heads from the prawns, the head of the spiny lobster—the latter cut into four—and the bones and trimmings from the sole into a small saucepan with 2 ladles of water and a little salt. Simmer for 15 minutes and then boil rapidly to reduce.

3 Pour the fumet through a strainer with a fine mesh and leave to cool. Add the soy sauce, saké, and sugar. Stir well and pour into four individual bowls. Before serving sprinkle with the grated horseradish and ginger.

4 Cut the fillets of sole into long strips; clean and slice the scallops. Cut the meat from the spiny lobster into slices.

5 Wash the vegetables. Dice the pepper and carrot; string the beans and leave whole.

6 Beat two egg yolks with a ladle of cold water in a bowl and work in the flour using a whisk.

7 Dip the pieces of fish and vegetables in the batter before frying.

8 Heat enough oil in a large cast-iron frying pan or wok and, keeping the temperature constant, deep fry the fish and vegetables in batches. Season with salt and pepper and serve very hot. Each person dips a selection of fried fish and vegetables into the soy sauce.

Bouillabaisse

Preparation: 2 hours

1.2 kg/2¾ lb assorted
  fish (scorpion fish,
  monkfish, gurnard,
  eel, Dublin Bay
  prawns)
1 leek
1 onion

150 ml/5 fl oz oil
pinch saffron threads
salt and black pepper
1 clove garlic
2 large tomatoes
400 g/14 oz mussels,
  cleaned
4 slices toasted bread
1 tbsp parsley

1   Remove the scales, clean and fillet the fish; cut into chunks, removing the head.

2   Prepare the fumet (page 181).

3   Finely chop the leek and onion; cook gently for 5 minutes in 5 tablespoons oil in a large saucepan. Add the fish and Dublin Bay prawns, mixed herbs, saffron, salt and pepper, and cover with the fumet.

4   Simmer gently for 5 minutes, then add the remaining oil, the crushed clove of garlic and the tomatoes, seeded, skinned, and chopped. Cook for another 10 minutes.

5   Remove the pieces of fish carefully and keep warm. Strain the stock. Place the mussels in a saucepan over high heat for 5 minutes until the shells open. Pour the stock over the fish and mussels, sprinkle with chopped parsley, and serve with slices of toasted bread.

Suggested menu

Seafood salad
Bouillabaisse
Calvados sorbet

Suggested wines

Riesling Renano dei Colli Orientali del Friuli, Ischia Bianco (Italy); Sancerre (France); Californian Chardonnay (U.S.A.); Pinot Riesling (Australia).

Fish soup with rice

Preparation: 1 hour
20 minutes

1 carrot
1 small onion
1 kg/2¼ lb fish
  trimmings (heads,
  tails, bones,
  preferably sole)

bouquet garni
salt
50 g/2 oz rice
2 eggs
juice of ¾ lemon
1 vegetable stock
  cube
pepper

1   Chop the carrot and onion and place in a saucepan with the fish trimmings and bouquet garni. Add 1 litre/1¾ pints water and salt to taste. Cover and simmer gently for 10 minutes, stirring occasionally.

2   Add another 1 litre/1¾ pints water and simmer for a further 20 minutes.

3   Strain the fumet, pressing to obtain as much liquid as possible, and boil for 15 minutes to reduce.

4   Add the rice and cook for 15 minutes or until tender.

5   Beat together the eggs, lemon juice, and a ladle of stock in a bowl. Add salt and pepper.

6   Pour the egg mixture into the soup and simmer gently for 3 minutes, stirring constantly. Do not allow to boil.

7   Remove from the heat, cover, and leave to stand for 1 minute before serving.

Suggested menu

Fish soup with rice
Braised sturgeon
Chestnut truffles

Suggested wines

Gavi, Trebbiano di Romagna (Italy); Muscadet (France); Californian Johannisberg Riesling (U.S.A.); Moselle Riesling (Germany).

Fish couscous

Preparation: 2¼ hours

1 kg/2¼ lb assorted
   fish (scorpion fish,
   grey mullet,
   gurnard or other)
1 onion
1 clove garlic

1 large ripe tomato
300 ml/10 fl oz oil
1 tbsp parsley
1 bay leaf
salt
pepper
150 g/5 oz couscous
pinch nutmeg
pinch cinnamon

Suggested menu

Soused herrings
Fish couscous
Lemon soufflé

Suggested wines

Sauvignon del Collio, Regaleali Bianco (Italy);
Sancerre (France); Californian Chardonnay
(U.S.A.); Rhine Riesling (Germany).

1   Clean the fish, rinse well, and drain. Slice the onion finely. Chop the garlic. Peel the tomato, remove and discard the seeds, and chop coarsely.

2   Heat 200 ml/7 fl oz oil in a large saucepan. Add the garlic, chopped parsley, bay leaf and finely sliced onion, and brown for 2 minutes. Add the tomato and cook for a further 2 minutes.

3   Place the fish in the saucepan, with the largest on the bottom. Pour over 1.5 litres/2½ pints water, season with salt and pepper, and simmer for 5 minutes.

4   Remove the fish and keep warm. Strain the fumet and pour three-quarters into the bottom of a couscous pan.

5   Place the couscous steamer on top of the pan. (In the absence of a special steamer use a colander lined with muslin.) Place the couscous inside, pour over the remaining oil, stir, and cover tightly to prevent steam escaping during cooking.

6   Place a weight on the lid and simmer gently for 20 minutes. During cooking the couscous will absorb the flavour of the fumet.

7   Pour the couscous into a frying pan, stir in some of the reserved fumet, and leave to stand for 1 hour. Add more fumet as the couscous expands and absorbs the liquid, and stir with a wooden spoon.

8   Arrange the couscous on a warm serving dish and pour over the cooking juices. Season with pepper, nutmeg, and cinnamon. Add salt if necessary. Skin and fillet the fish and arrange on top of the couscous.

Paella valenciana

Preparation: 1 hour 40 minutes

½ onion
1 green or yellow pepper, 2 tomatoes
½ small chicken
125 g/4 oz pork tenderloin
125 ml/4 fl oz oil, 1 clove garlic

125 g/4 oz spicy sausage
salt and pepper,
1 sachet saffron powder,
1 bay leaf
600 ml/1 pint stock or water
4 Dublin Bay prawns
16 mussels
125 g/4 oz pilaf rice
125 g/4 oz shelled peas
pinch chilli powder

Suggested menu

Prawn cocktail
Paella valenciana
Hazelnut ice cream log

Suggested wines

Ribolla dei Colli Orientali del Friuli, Pinot Grigio
dell'Alto Adige (Italy); Chassagne Montrachet
(France); Californian Chardonnay (U.S.A.);
Chenin Blanc (South Africa).

1 Chop the onion. Char the pepper over a flame; plunge into cold water and rub off the skin. Discard the seeds and cut the pepper into thin strips. Peel the tomatoes, remove the seeds, and chop. Cut the chicken into pieces and dice the pork.

2 Heat 3 tablespoons oil in a frying pan and brown the chicken and pork for 10 minutes. Remove and set aside. Put the sausage in the same pan, prick with a fork and fry for 10 minutes. Set aside with the meat.

3 Add 2 tablespoons oil to the pan and fry the onion and crushed garlic briefly. Remove the garlic as soon as it begins to brown. When the onion begins to brown add the tomatoes. Add salt to taste and cook for 10 minutes.

4 Place the scrubbed mussels in a pan, cover, and cook over high heat for 5 minutes until the shells open.

5 Place the chicken, pork, sausage, and bay leaf in a saucepan with 600 ml/1 pint stock and simmer for 15 minutes.

6 Cook the Dublin Bay prawns in boiling salted water for 3 minutes. Drain.

7 Heat 3 tablespoons oil in a large paella pan or cast-iron frying pan and brown the rice, stirring with a wooden spoon. Gradually stir in the cooking liquid from the meat, the strips of pepper, and the shelled peas. Dissolve the saffron in a little warm water and stir into the rice. Cook for about 15 minutes or until the rice is tender.

8 Stir in all the remaining ingredients. Mix well and place in a hot oven for 5 minutes before serving.

Seafood mixed fry

Preparation: 1 hour

250 g/9 oz small red
  mullet
400 g/14 oz baby
  squid or cuttlefish
250 g/9 oz cooked
  prawns

175 g/6 oz whitebait
plain flour
oil for deep frying
salt
parsley
slices of lemon

1   Clean the red mullet.
Rinse the squid, prawns,
and whitebait, and drain.

2   Cut the tentacles off
the squid or cuttlefish and
cut the bodies into rings.

3   Coat all the fish lightly
with seasoned flour.

4   Heat plenty of oil until
it begins to smoke and fry
the mullet on both sides
for 4 minutes. Remove, set
aside and keep hot. Deep
fry the squid or cuttlefish
for 3 minutes.

5   Fry the whitebait for 3
minutes, then fry the
prawns for 4 minutes.

6   Drain all the fish on
kitchen paper and serve at
once, garnished with
parsley and slices of
lemon.

Suggested menu

Sea date soup
Seafood mixed fry
Zabaglione

Suggested wines

Spumante Champenois dell'Oltrepò Pavese,
Vermentino (Italy); Graves Blanc (France);
Californian Chardonnay (U.S.A.); Pinot Riesling
(Australia).

Cioppino

Preparation: 1 hour

400 g/14 oz mussels,
  cleaned and scrubbed
1 spiny lobster
salt
225 g/8 oz prawns
1 450-g/1-lb sea bass
50 ml/2 fl oz oil

½ onion
1 clove garlic
½ green pepper
2 ripe tomatoes
1 tsp tomato purée
125 ml/4 fl oz white
  wine
pepper
1 tbsp parsley

1   Place the mussels in a saucepan over high heat for 3 minutes or until the shells open. Strain and reserve the liquid. Remove from their shells.

2   Cook the spiny lobster in boiling salted water for 10 minutes. Leave to cool, then cut the flesh into pieces.

3   Peel the prawns. Crush the heads and simmer for 10 minutes in 400 ml/ 14 fl oz water, then strain.

4   Remove the scales, clean and fillet the sea bass and cut into pieces.

5   Heat the oil in a frying pan; add the chopped onion and garlic, and the pepper, cut into pieces. Cook for 4 minutes. Add the tomatoes and tomato purée, the wine, and the reserved liquid from the mussels and from the prawns. Season with salt and pepper, lower the heat, and simmer, covered, for 10 minutes.

6   Add the pieces of sea bass, cover and cook for a further 10 minutes. Add the prawns and cook for 3 minutes, then add the lobster, mussels, and parsley. Cover and cook for 2 minutes before serving.

Suggested menu

Sardines in 'saòr'
Cioppino
Ladies' kisses

Suggested wines

Terlano dell'Alto Adige, Vermentino (Italy); Sancerre (France); Californian Gewürztraminer (U.S.A.); Rhine Sylvaner (Germany).

Saltwater fish

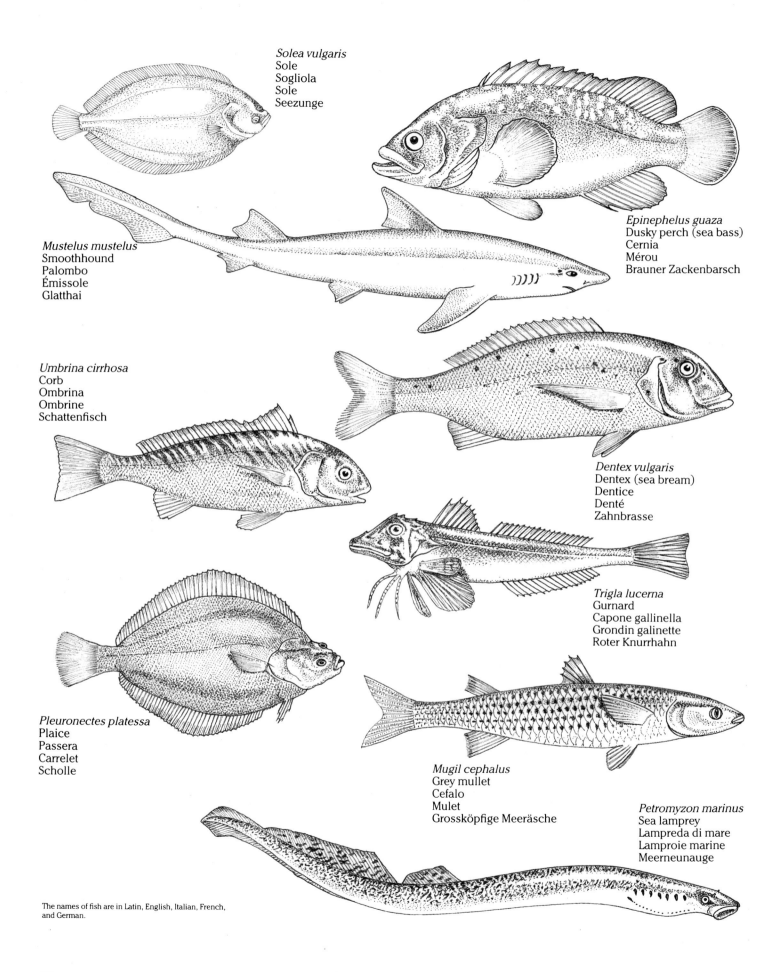

Solea vulgaris
Sole
Sogliola
Sole
Seezunge

Epinephelus guaza
Dusky perch (sea bass)
Cernia
Mérou
Brauner Zackenbarsch

Mustelus mustelus
Smoothhound
Palombo
Émissole
Glatthai

Umbrina cirrhosa
Corb
Ombrina
Ombrine
Schattenfisch

Dentex vulgaris
Dentex (sea bream)
Dentice
Denté
Zahnbrasse

Trigla lucerna
Gurnard
Capone gallinella
Grondin galinette
Roter Knurrhahn

Pleuronectes platessa
Plaice
Passera
Carrelet
Scholle

Mugil cephalus
Grey mullet
Cefalo
Mulet
Grossköpfige Meeräsche

Petromyzon marinus
Sea lamprey
Lampreda di mare
Lamproie marine
Meerneunauge

The names of fish are in Latin, English, Italian, French, and German.

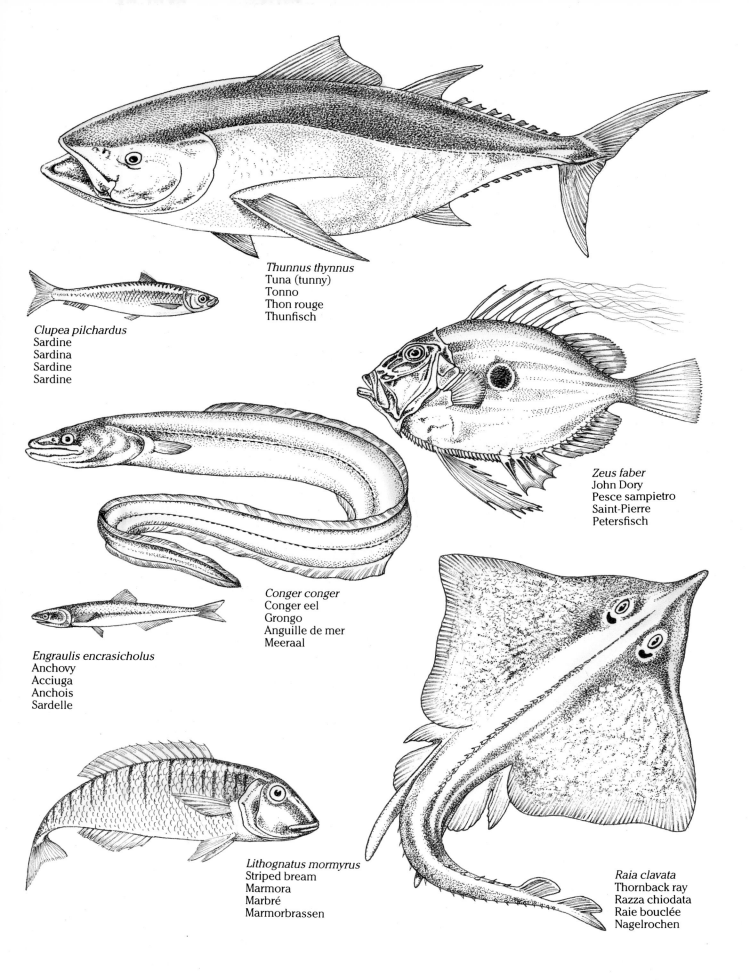

Thunnus thynnus
Tuna (tunny)
Tonno
Thon rouge
Thunfisch

Clupea pilchardus
Sardine
Sardina
Sardine
Sardine

Zeus faber
John Dory
Pesce sampietro
Saint-Pierre
Petersfisch

Conger conger
Conger eel
Grongo
Anguille de mer
Meeraal

Engraulis encrasicholus
Anchovy
Acciuga
Anchois
Sardelle

Lithognatus mormyrus
Striped bream
Marmora
Marbré
Marmorbrassen

Raia clavata
Thornback ray
Razza chiodata
Raie bouclée
Nagelrochen

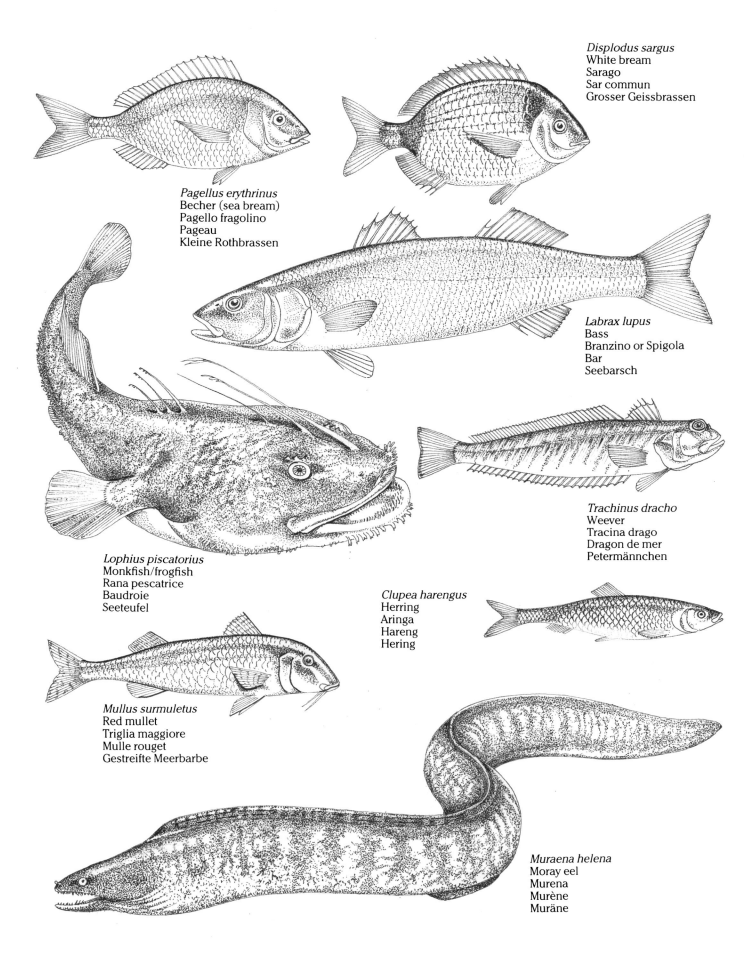

Displodus sargus
White bream
Sarago
Sar commun
Grosser Geissbrassen

Pagellus erythrinus
Becher (sea bream)
Pagello fragolino
Pageau
Kleine Rothbrassen

Labrax lupus
Bass
Branzino or Spigola
Bar
Seebarsch

Lophius piscatorius
Monkfish/frogfish
Rana pescatrice
Baudroie
Seeteufel

Trachinus dracho
Weever
Tracina drago
Dragon de mer
Petermännchen

Clupea harengus
Herring
Aringa
Hareng
Hering

Mullus surmuletus
Red mullet
Triglia maggiore
Mulle rouget
Gestreifte Meerbarbe

Muraena helena
Moray eel
Murena
Murène
Muräne

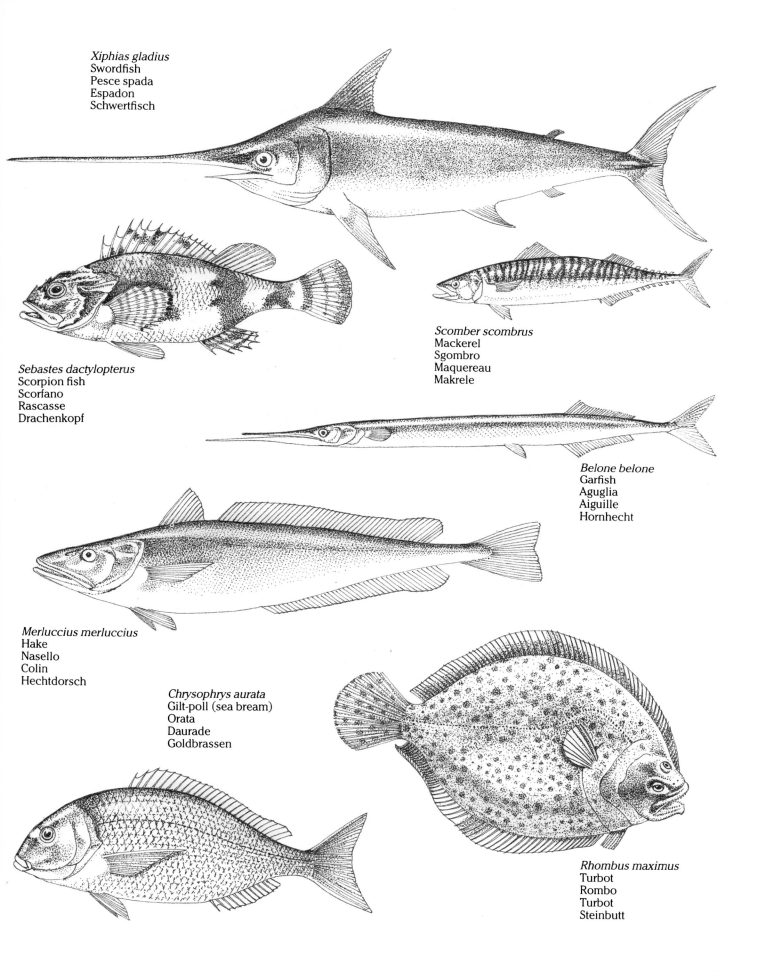

Xiphias gladius
Swordfish
Pesce spada
Espadon
Schwertfisch

Scomber scombrus
Mackerel
Sgombro
Maquereau
Makrele

Sebastes dactylopterus
Scorpion fish
Scorfano
Rascasse
Drachenkopf

Belone belone
Garfish
Aguglia
Aiguille
Hornhecht

Merluccius merluccius
Hake
Nasello
Colin
Hechtdorsch

Chrysophrys aurata
Gilt-poll (sea bream)
Orata
Daurade
Goldbrassen

Rhombus maximus
Turbot
Rombo
Turbot
Steinbutt

Skate au beurre noir

Preparation: 1 hour
(+ 2 hours for
soaking the skate)

1.2 kg/2¾ lb wing of
 skate
salt and pepper
1 onion
2 carrots

4 sprigs parsley
50 ml/2 fl oz wine
 vinegar
10 peppercorns
1 bay leaf
1 tbsp chopped
 parsley
1 tbsp capers
80 g/3 oz butter

Suggested menu

Salade niçoise
Skate au beurre noir
Zabaglione

Suggested wines

Pinot Champenois di Franciacorta, Pinot Bianco
del Collio (Italy); Champagne (France);
Californian Blanc de Blancs (U.S.A.); Blanc
Fumé (South Africa).

1   Buy ready-cleaned skate or have it cleaned and skinned by the fishmonger. Wash under cold running water and leave to soak in salted water for 2 hours.

2   Slice the onion and carrots.

3   Cut the skate into four.

4   Place the skate in a wide frying pan with the onion, carrot, parsley, 3 tablespoons of wine vinegar, salt, peppercorns, and bay leaf. Cover with cold water, bring to the boil, and simmer very gently for 15 minutes.

5   Drain the skate and arrange on a serving dish.

6   Sprinkle with salt, pepper, chopped parsley, and crushed capers. Keep warm.

7   Melt the butter in a small saucepan and heat until it turns golden brown. Take care not to burn it. Pour the butter over the skate. Return the pan to the heat, warm the remaining wine vinegar, and pour over the fish. Serve immediately with boiled new potatoes topped with butter and parsley.

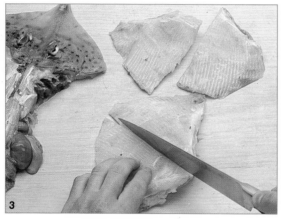

Soused herrings

Preparation: 40 minutes (+ 12 hours for marinating the herrings)

2 carrots
1 onion
300 ml/10 fl oz white wine

200 ml/7 fl oz wine vinegar
2 bay leaves
2 sprigs thyme
6 white peppercorns
3 cloves
salt
800 g/1¾ lb fresh herrings
1 tbsp parsley

1   Prepare the marinade: finely chop the carrots and onion. Place in a saucepan with the wine, wine vinegar, 1 bay leaf, 1 sprig thyme, the peppercorns, cloves, and a pinch of salt. Bring to the boil and simmer gently for 10 minutes.

2   Clean the herrings: remove the scales, backbone, heads, and tails. Wash and pat dry with kitchen paper.

3   Place the herrings in a flameproof casserole, sprinkle with the chopped parsley, 1 crumbled bay leaf and a sprig of thyme.

4   Pour the marinade over the herrings and cook over moderate heat for 5 minutes.

5   Allow to cool, cover, and refrigerate for 12 hours.

6   Remove from the refrigerator at least 2 hours before serving.

Suggested menu

Soused herrings
Skate au beurre noir
Ladies' kisses

Suggested wines

Terlano dell'Alto Adige, Greco di Tufo (Italy); Meursault (France); Californian Gewürztraminer (U.S.A.); Chenin Blanc (New Zealand).

Herring salad

Preparation: 1 hour
(+ 24 hours for
marinating the herrings)

4 salted herrings
2 potatoes, 2 beetroot
1 cooking apple
1 cucumber
125 g/4 oz cooked veal

½ onion, 2 tbsp oil
2 tbsp wine vinegar
pepper
3 hard-boiled eggs
½ tbsp mustard
salt
3 tbsp sour cream or
    plain yogurt
1 tbsp chopped dill

1   Soak the herrings for 24 hours in cold water, changing the water as often as possible.

2   Boil and dice the potatoes. Dice the beetroot, apple, cucumber, and veal. Chop the onion. Cut the heads off the herrings; open the fish flat, pressing along the backbone; remove and discard the backbone and skin. Cut the fish into pieces.

3   Place all the ingredients in a large bowl and season with 1 tablespoon wine vinegar. Sprinkle with pepper.

4   Push the hard-boiled eggs through a fine sieve into a small bowl. Mix together 1 tablespoon wine vinegar, the mustard, and a pinch of salt. Stir in the oil gradually and add the sour cream last.

5   Pour the mixture over the herrings, stir carefully, and sprinkle with chopped dill and the sieved egg yolks. Cover and refrigerate for 3 hours. Garnish with hard-boiled eggs and lettuce.

Suggested menu

Herring salad
Manhattan clam chowder
Wild strawberries and ice cream

Suggested wines

Pinot Champenois di Franciacorta, Pinot Grigio dell'Alto Adige (Italy); Chassagne Montrachet (France); Californian Gewürztraminer (U.S.A.); Rhine Sylvaner (Germany).

Rollmops

Preparation: 1 hour
(+ 4 hours for
soaking and 3 days
for marinating)

4 fresh herrings
50 g/2 oz salt
300 ml/10 fl oz white
   wine vinegar

2 bay leaves
8 black peppercorns
1 tsp mixed spices
   (coriander, juniper
   berries, fresh dill)
2 onions
2 gherkins

1   Cut the head and tail from the herrings; open the fish flat and remove the bones and entrails.

2   Dissolve the salt in 500 ml/18 fl oz water and leave the herrings to soak for at least 4 hours. Turn them every 30 minutes. Drain and dry the fillets.

3   Bring the vinegar to the boil in a saucepan. Add the bay leaf, peppercorns, and spices, remove from the heat and leave to cool.

4   Slice one onion and the gherkins and wrap each fillet around a slice of onion and gherkin.

5   Place the rolled fillets in a glass or earthenware jar and place the remaining slices of onion and gherkin between them. Pour in the vinegar, cover, and leave to marinate in a cool place for 3 to 4 days.

6   Slice the remaining onion and serve raw with the rollmops. Serve with slices of brown bread or rye bread and butter.

Suggested menu

Rollmops
Cuttlefish with peas
Apricot soufflé

Suggested wines

Pinot Grigio dell'Alto Adige, Regaleali Bianco (Italy); Bourgogne Blanc (France); Californian Pinot Blanc (U.S.A.); Chardonnay (Australia).

Taramasalata

Preparation: 20 minutes (+ 2 hours for soaking the roe and 2 hours for refrigeration)

125 g/4 oz smoked cod's roe

50 g/2 oz white bread
1 onion
1 egg yolk
125 ml/4 fl oz oil
½ lemon
salt
olives
pitta bread

1   Soak the 'tarama' or cod's roe in water for 2 hours to remove excess salt.

2   Remove the crust from the bread and soak in water. Squeeze very dry.

3   In a blender or food processor mix together the soaked and squeezed bread, the onion, egg yolk, and 3 tablespoons of oil. Blend well, and add the roe and remaining oil gradually. Blend thoroughly, adding the lemon juice last.

4   Adjust the seasoning and pour the mixture into a mould or individual ramekins. Refrigerate for 2 hours.

5   Serve garnished with black olives and slices of toasted bread or pitta bread.

Suggested menu

Taramasalata
Braised sturgeon
Strawberries in Champagne

Suggested wines

Spumante Champenois del Trentino, Vernaccia di San Gimignano (Italy); Meursault (France); Californian Chardonnay (U.S.A.); Chenin Blanc (Australia).

Grey mullet Bulgarian style

Preparation: 40 minutes

2 grey mullet, total weight 1 kg/2¼ lb
salt
pepper
2 tbsp fresh dill

2 tbsp chopped parsley
125 ml/4 fl oz brandy

1   Remove the scales from the fish; clean, rinse, and pat dry.

2   Sprinkle with salt and pepper.

3   Mix together the chopped dill and parsley.

4   Grill or barbecue the fish for about 20 minutes, turning frequently.

5   Place the fish in a large frying pan and sprinkle with the chopped herbs.

6   Heat the brandy, pour over the fish, and flame. Serve at once.

Suggested menu

Macaroni with fresh sardines and dill
Grey mullet Bulgarian style
Aniseed and almond biscuits

Suggested wines

Corvo di Salaparuta, Frascati (Italy); Pouilly-Fuissé (France); Californian Pinot Blanc (U.S.A.); Moselle Riesling (Germany).

Pompano en papillote

Preparation: 1 hour

2 pompano, total
  weight 1 kg/2¼ lb
400 ml/14 fl oz fumet
  (page 181)
300 ml/10 fl oz dry
  white wine
80 g/3 oz butter

225 g/8 oz prawns
1 tbsp parsley
2 onions
40 g/1½ oz plain flour
Cayenne pepper
salt
1–2 tbsp single cream
225 g/8 oz cooked
  crabmeat

Suggested menu

Seafood salad
Pompano en papillote
Chestnut truffles

Suggested wines

Torgiano Bianco, Ischia Bianco (Italy); Pinot
d'Alsace (France); Californian Chenin Blanc
(U.S.A.); Rhine Sylvaner (Germany).

1 Clean and fillet the fish. Rinse and pat dry.

2 Place the fillets in a frying pan with half the fumet, the wine, and a little butter. Bring to a simmer and heat gently for 5 minutes.

3 Peel the prawns and remove the central black vein. Wash and pat dry with kitchen paper.

4 Melt 25 g/1 oz butter in a frying pan, add the prawns, and cook for 3 minutes. Sprinkle with chopped parsley.

5 Melt 25 g/1 oz butter in a saucepan, add the chopped onions, and fry for 5 minutes; add the flour and stir constantly with a whisk for 1 minute.

6 Add the remaining fumet; bring to the boil, lower the heat, and simmer for 3 minutes. Stir in a little Cayenne pepper, salt, and the cream.

7 Cut out 8 foil heart shapes and butter 4 of them. Place a fillet of fish, a quarter of the prawns, and a quarter of the crabmeat on each.

8 Spoon over a little of the sauce and cover with a piece of foil. Seal the edges well. Place the *papillotes* on a baking tray in a preheated oven at 200°C/400°F/mark 6 for 8 minutes. Serve immediately.

Fillets of sole à la normande

Preparation: 50 minutes (+ 2 hours for cleaning the mussels)

450 g/1 lb mussels
125 g/4 oz prawns
300 ml/10 fl oz fumet (page 181)

175 g/6 oz mushrooms
50 g/2 oz butter
4 fillets of sole
225 ml/8 fl oz white wine
salt and pepper
25 g/1 oz plain flour
3 egg yolks
juice of 1 lemon

1   Heat the mussels in a covered saucepan for 3 minutes. Remove from the shells; strain and reserve the liquor. Heat the prawns for 4 minutes in 50 ml/ 2 fl oz fumet. Peel them, place the shells in the fumet, and simmer for 5 minutes. Strain the fumet.

2   Wash and slice the mushrooms. Heat for 10 minutes in 15 g/½ oz butter.

3   Place the fillets in a buttered ovenproof dish with the wine and 125 ml/ 4 fl oz fumet. Season.

Cover with buttered foil and bake at 170°C/325°F/ mark 3 for 8 minutes.

4   Pour the liquor into the remaining fumet and reduce over high heat.

5   Melt 25 g/1 oz butter, stir in the flour and cook for 1 minute. Add the fumet gradually and cook for 3 minutes. Beat the egg yolks and stir into the sauce. Add the remaining butter and lemon juice.

6   Transfer the fillets to another casserole. Sur-round with mushrooms, mussels and prawns; cover with sauce and place in the oven preheated to 200°C/400°F/ mark 6 for 5 minutes.

Suggested menu

Scallops in white wine
Fillets of sole à la normande
Aniseed and almond biscuits

Suggested wines

Spumante Champenois dell'Oltrepò Pavese, Terlano dell'Alto Adige (Italy); Champagne (France); Californian Sauvignon Blanc (U.S.A.); Moselle Riesling (Germany).

Fillets of sole Saint-Germain

Preparation: 1 hour

450 g/1 lb potatoes
125 g/4 oz clarified
   butter (page 181)
salt and pepper

800 g/1¾ lb sole
   fillets
dried breadcrumbs

Serve with: Béarnaise
sauce (page 182)

1   Peel and dice the potatoes.

2   Melt half the butter in a frying pan and sauté the potatoes until golden brown. Drain on kitchen paper, sprinkle with salt, and keep warm.

3   Sprinkle the fillets of sole with salt and brush with the remaining melted butter. Dip in breadcrumbs, pressing well to ensure that they are evenly coated.

4   Preheat the oven to 180°C/350°F/mark 4 and place the fillets directly onto the top rungs. Cook for a total of 8 minutes, turning the fillets halfway through. Alternatively, cook on a barbecue or grill.

5   Sprinkle the fillets with pepper and arrange on a heated serving dish with the sautéed potatoes.

6   Serve with Béarnaise sauce heated in a *bain-marie*.

Suggested menu

Clam fritters
Fillets of sole Saint-Germain
Pear flan

Suggested wines

Sylvaner dell'Alto Adige, Frascati (Italy); Pinot d'Alsace (France); Californian Pinot Blanc (U.S.A.); Sauvignon Blanc (South Africa).

Ceviche

(Fillets of sole Peruvian style)

Preparation: 40 minutes (+ 4 hours for marinating the sole)

600 g/1¼ lb sole fillets
2 lemons
½ onion
1 clove garlic
½ tbsp chopped parsley
2 large ripe beef tomatoes
1 tsp chilli powder
3 tbsp oil
salt

1   Place the fillets in a deep dish and pour over the lemon juice. Refrigerate for 4 hours, turning several times with a wooden spoon. The fish will become white and firm.

2   Chop the onion, garlic, and parsley very finely.

3   Peel the tomatoes, remove the seeds, and dice.

4   Mix together in a bowl the onion, garlic, parsley, tomatoes, chilli powder, and oil. Sprinkle with salt, then turn these ingredients into a serving dish.

5   Drain the fillets (reserve the lemon juice), cut into fairly large pieces and arrange decoratively on top of the seasoned tomatoes.

6   Sprinkle with a little of the reserved lemon juice and garnish with parsley.

Suggested menu

Ceviche
Grilled or barbecued turbot
Raspberries with zabaglione

Suggested wines

Gavi, Frascati (Italy); Chablis (France); Californian Chenin Blanc (U.S.A.); Rhine Riesling (Germany).

Sole with aniseed sauce

Preparation: 20 minutes

600 g/1¾ lb sole fillets
6 tbsp oil
plain flour
2 shallots
1 clove garlic
1 tsp green aniseed
1 small red chilli pepper
2 tbsp white wine vinegar
3 tsp sugar
1 anchovy or 1 tbsp anchovy paste
salt

1   Cut the fillets into 5-cm/2-in pieces.

2   Heat the oil in a frying pan. Dip the fillets in flour and fry over moderate heat for 4 minutes on each side.

3   Finely chop the shallots and garlic.

4   Finely chop the aniseed and cut the chilli pepper into fine rings, discarding the seeds.

5   Remove the fish from the frying pan and keep warm. Add the chopped shallots and garlic to the pan and fry for 2 minutes. Stir in the vinegar, sugar, aniseed, chilli pepper, and a few tablespoons water. Simmer for 2 minutes.

6   Finely chop the anchovy and stir into the mixture. Simmer for 5 minutes. Adjust seasoning. Return the fillets to the pan to heat through.

Suggested menu

Scallops in white wine
Sole with aniseed sauce
Lemon tart

Suggested wines

Vernaccia di San Gimignano, Sylvaner dell'Alto Adige (Italy); Sancerre (France); Californian Gewürztraminer (U.S.A.); Rhine Riesling (South Africa).

Sole à la meunière

Preparation: 20 minutes

4 sole, total weight 1 kg/2¼ lb
50 g/2 oz butter

2 tbsp plain flour
salt
1 tbsp lemon juice
1 tbsp chopped parsley

1   Clean the sole; remove the skin from the dark side and gently scrape the white side.

2   Melt half the butter in a large frying pan. Dip the sole in flour and shake off the excess.

3   Gently fry the sole in the butter for 6 to 7 minutes, turning once with a fish slice, and season with salt.

4   When the sole are golden brown, transfer to a heated serving dish and sprinkle with a few drops of lemon juice and finely chopped parsley.

5   In the same frying pan heat the remaining butter until golden brown and foaming. Pour over the sole and serve immediately.

Suggested menu

Prawn risotto
Sole à la meunière
Apricot soufflé

Suggested wines

Gavi, Pinot Grigio dell'Alto Adige (Italy); Chablis (France); Californian Chenin Blanc (U.S.A.); Chardonnay (Australia).

Sole alla parmigiana

Preparation: 30 minutes

4 sole, total weight
  1 kg/2¼ lb
plain flour
3 tbsp oil

salt
4 tbsp dried
  breadcrumbs
4 tbsp grated
  Parmesan cheese
40 g/1½ oz butter

1   Remove the skin from the dark side of the sole and gently scrape the white side.

2   Dip the sole in flour.

3   Heat the oil in a frying pan. Lay the fish in the pan, sprinkle with salt and cook for 2 minutes each side. Drain.

4   Mix together the breadcrumbs and Parmesan and press on to each fish.

5   Melt the butter in an ovenproof rectangular casserole dish. Lay the fish side by side in the dish and cook in a preheated oven at 200°C/ 400°F/mark 6 until lightly browned, turning once.

Suggested menu

Spaghetti with spiny lobster
Sole alla parmigiana
Flambéed pineapple

Suggested wines

Riesling dell'Oltrepò Pavese, Orvieto (Italy); Chablis (France); Californian Chardonnay (U.S.A.); Müller Thurgau (New Zealand).

Sea bass with 'tarator' sauce

Preparation: 40 minutes
(+ 2 hours for
marinating the sea bass)

4 sea bass steaks, total
  weight 1 kg/2¼ lb
salt
2 lemons, 4 tbsp oil
fresh parsley

black olives and
  radishes for garnish
Sauce:
2 slices white bread,
  crusts removed
40 walnuts, shelled
½ lemon, 1 clove garlic
salt and pepper
2 tbsp sesame paste

1. Sprinkle the steaks with a teaspoon of salt and the juice of one lemon and refrigerate for 2 hours.

2. Prepare the 'tarator' sauce: soak the bread in water for a few minutes.

3. Squeeze the bread and place in a liquidizer together with the shelled walnuts, juice of ½ lemon, the crushed garlic, salt and pepper, and blend for 3 minutes.

4. The mixture should be smooth and thick. Add the sesame paste and blend for another minute.

5. Rinse and pat dry the fish steaks and place on an oiled baking tray.

6. Bake in a preheated oven (200°C/400°F/mark 6) for 20 minutes, turning occasionally and brushing with oil every 5 minutes. Leave to cool and cover with a little 'tarator' sauce. Serve garnished with black olives, slices of lemon, parsley, and radishes. Serve the remaining sauce separately.

Suggested menu

Moules marinière
Sea bass with 'tarator' sauce
Floating islands

Suggested wines

Pinot dell'Oltrepò Pavese, Frascati (Italy); Pouilly-Fuissé (France); Californian Gewürztraminer (U.S.A.); Rhine Riesling (Germany).

Sea bass with orange sauce

Preparation: 40 minutes

800 g/1¾ lb sea bass
6 tbsp oil

50 g/2 oz plain flour
salt
40 g/1½ oz butter
200 ml/7 fl oz milk
3 oranges

Suggested menu

Spaghetti with tuna
Sea bass with orange sauce
Apricot soufflé

Suggested wines

Pinot Champenois di Franciacorta, Sauvignon
del Collio (Italy); Pouilly-Fuissé (France);
Californian Pinot Blanc (U.S.A.); Chardonnay
(South Africa).

1   Cut the sea bass into steaks 2 cm/¾ in thick.

2   Heat the oil in a frying pan. Coat the steaks lightly in flour and fry for 10 minutes over medium heat, turning after 5 minutes. Season with salt, drain, and keep warm.

3   Melt the butter in a clean pan, stir in the flour and cook the *roux* for 2 minutes.

4   Stir in the milk gradually and cook for 5 minutes.

5   Squeeze two oranges.

6   Add the orange juice to the white sauce and cook for a further 5 minutes, stirring constantly. Add salt to taste.

7   Pour the sauce over the fish steaks and cook gently for another 5 minutes.

8   Wash the remaining orange and, without peeling, cut it into fine slices. Cut each slice in half and use for garnish.

Sea bass en croûte

Preparation: 1 hour
(+ 30 minutes for the
pastry to stand)

1 1-kg/2¼-lb sea bass
fresh tarragon
fresh chervil
salt and pepper

400 g/14 oz puff
  pastry (page 181)
2 egg yolks
parsley

Serve with: beurre blanc
(page 181)

1   Clean, rinse, and skin the sea bass, leaving head and tail intact. Make a cut along the backbone and place a piece of tarragon and chervil inside, as well as in the belly cavity. Season with salt and pepper.

2   Prepare the pastry and roll out into two rectangles 5 cm/2 in bigger than the fish.

3   Lay one rectangle on a buttered baking tray, place the fish on top, and cover with the second piece. Press the edges firmly together. Refrigerate for 30 minutes.

4   Remove the fish from the refrigerator and trim the excess pastry from around the edge. Use to make fins, eyes, etc.

5   Brush the pastry with the beaten egg yolks. Bake in a preheated oven at 200°C/400°F/mark 6 for 10 minutes. Reduce the heat to 180°C/350°F/mark 4 and bake for 20 minutes. Transfer to a heated serving dish.

6   Garnish with parsley. Serve with beurre blanc.

Suggested menu

Clam chowder
Sea bass en croûte
Almond squares

Suggested wines

Tocai del Collio, Soave (Italy); Montrachet (France); Californian Chardonnay (U.S.A.); Chenin Blanc (New Zealand).

Spaghetti with tuna

Preparation: 20 minutes

1 large onion
5 tbsp oil
salt and pepper
200 g/7 oz tinned tuna
250 g/9 oz spaghetti
1 tbsp chopped parsley

1   Finely chop the onion.

2   Heat the oil in a frying pan and fry the onion for 1 minute. Add salt and 125 ml/4 fl oz water and cook for 4 minutes.

3   Add the drained and flaked tuna and cook for 3 minutes.

4   Cook the spaghetti in plenty of boiling salted water for 10 to 12 minutes or until *al dente*. Drain well.

5   Pour the spaghetti into the frying pan with the tuna and onions. Sprinkle with chopped parsley, salt, and pepper.

6   Toss well and serve immediately.

Suggested menu

Spaghetti with tuna
Sea bream niçoise
Hazelnut ice cream log

Suggested wines

Verdicchio dei Castelli di Jesi, Soave (Italy); Chablis (France); Californian Chardonnay (U.S.A.); Müller Thurgau (New Zealand).

Tuna steaks with capers and anchovies

Preparation: 1 hour

4 tbsp wine vinegar
4 tuna steaks, total
   weight 1 kg/2¼ lb
6 tbsp oil
50 g/2 oz butter
1 onion
bunch parsley

1 bay leaf
salt and black pepper
125 ml/4 fl oz Marsala
1 vegetable stock cube
4 thick slices white
   bread
2 anchovy fillets
1 lemon
2 tbsp capers

Suggested menu

Prawn cocktail
Tuna steaks with capers and anchovies
Flambéed apricots

Suggested wines

Orvieto, Soave (Italy); Meursault (France);
Californian Chenin Blanc (U.S.A.); Chardonnay
(Australia).

1   Fill a frying pan halfway with salted water and add 4 tbsp wine vinegar.

2   Bring to the boil, add the tuna steaks, and simmer for 3 minutes. Drain and pat dry.

3   In a separate pan heat half the oil and butter and add the finely chopped onion, the parsley (rinsed and tied), and the crumbled bay leaf.

4   Place the tuna steaks in this pan and fry for 4 minutes on each side. Season with salt and pepper.

5   Stir in the Marsala and a ladle of vegetable stock.

6   Gently heat the remaining oil and butter in a separate frying pan and brown the slices of bread. Transfer to a serving dish.

7   Place a tuna steak on each slice of bread and keep warm.

8   Remove and discard the parsley and add the chopped anchovy fillets and lemon juice to the sauce. Simmer for a few minutes, then pass through a fine sieve. Reheat the sauce and add the well-drained capers. Pour over the tuna steaks.

Tuna Charterhouse style

Preparation: 1 hour

4 tuna steaks, total
    weight 1 kg/2¼ lb
salt and pepper
1 lemon
4 anchovy fillets

1 onion
3 carrots
4 tbsp oil
4 lettuce hearts
bunch sorrel
225 ml/8 fl oz white
    wine

1   Place the tuna steaks
in boiling salted water
acidulated with the lemon
juice and boil for 1 minute.

2   Drain and dry the tuna
steaks. Make several
incisions in each and insert
the pieces of anchovy.

3   Finely slice the onion
and cut the carrots into
rounds. Pour the oil into a
large pan, add the onion
and carrots, season with
salt and pepper, and fry for
4 minutes. Place the tuna
steaks on top of the
vegetables, cover and
cook for 3 minutes. Add
salt, turn the steaks, and
cook for a further
3 minutes.

4   Blanch the lettuce
hearts in boiling salted
water for 2 minutes.

5   Drain and squeeze the
lettuce hearts and place
on top of the tuna steaks.
Rinse and dry the sorrel
and place in the centre of
the steaks. Cook for 4
minutes over moderate
heat.

6   Sprinkle with salt and
pepper and white wine;
cover and simmer for
about 20 minutes. Serve
each steak with a
selection of the vegetables
and garnish with a little
fresh sorrel.

Suggested menu

Coquilles Saint-Jacques à la provençale
Tuna Charterhouse style
Raspberry Bavarian cream

Suggested wines

Pinot Grigio dell'Alto Adige, Pinot Champenois
di Franciacorta (Italy); Pinot d'Alsace (France);
Californian Johannisberg Riesling (U.S.A.);
Sauvignon Blanc (South Africa).

Salade niçoise

Preparation: 1 hour
(+ 30 minutes for
soaking the
anchovies)

50 g/2 oz salted or
    tinned anchovies
salt
225 g/8 oz potatoes

225 g/8 oz French beans
2 hard-boiled eggs
225 g/8 oz tomatoes
1 lettuce
225 g/8 oz tinned tuna
5 tbsp oil
3 tbsp vinegar
50 g/2 oz small black
    olives

1   Rinse the salted anchovies under cold running water; divide each one in half, remove the backbone and leave to soak for 30 minutes.

2   Boil the potatoes in their skins in salted water for approximately 20 minutes. Leave to cool; peel and slice thinly.

3   String the beans and boil in salted water for about 8 minutes. Drain and leave to cool.

4   Cut each egg into four and slice the tomatoes.

5   Rinse and dry the lettuce leaves and cut into shreds. Drain the tuna and flake.

6   Prepare a vinaigrette by beating together the oil, vinegar, and a little salt.

7   Place the lettuce, beans, and potatoes in a bowl and dress with half the vinaigrette. Toss well.

8   Arrange on a serving platter and garnish with the hard-boiled eggs, tomatoes, anchovies, and olives. Pour over the remaining vinaigrette.

Suggested menu

Salade niçoise
Skate au beurre noir
Raspberry Bavarian cream

Suggested wines

Gavi, Soave (Italy); Meursault (France); Californian Chenin Blanc (U.S.A.); Riesling (Australia).

Anchovies with rice

Preparation: 1 hour
(+ 30 minutes for
soaking the sultanas)

250 g/9 oz basmati
 rice
salt
1 large onion
80 g/3 oz butter

1 tbsp sultanas
ground allspice
½ tsp powdered
 cinnamon
½ tsp sugar
800 g/1¾ lb fresh
 anchovies
1 tbsp pine nuts

1   Soak the rice for 30
minutes in warm salted
water.

2   Finely slice the onion
and brown gently in half
the butter.

3   Drain the rice and add
to the onion. Fry for 5
minutes, stirring
constantly.

4   Add a ladle of hot
water, the sultanas, plenty
of ground allspice, the
cinnamon, the sugar, and
salt. Cook for another 5
minutes.

5   Clean the anchovies,
remove the heads and
bones, and sprinkle with
salt.

6   Butter a large
ovenproof dish and cover
with a layer of anchovies.
Cover with the rice and the
remaining anchovies;
sprinkle with pine nuts,
dot with the remaining
butter and place in a
preheated oven at 180°C/
350°F/mark 4 for 10
minutes.

Suggested menu

Seafood salad
Anchovies with rice
Lemon soufflé

Suggested wines

Sylvaner dell'Alto Adige, Riesling dell'Oltrepò
Pavese (Italy); Montrachet (France); Californian
Gewürztraminer (U.S.A.); Müller Thurgau (New
Zealand).

Jansson's temptation

Preparation: 1 hour 10 minutes (+ 20 minutes for soaking the anchovies)

12 salted anchovies
450 g/1 lb potatoes

2 large onions
80 g/3 oz butter
2 tbsp oil
salt and pepper
225 ml/8 fl oz double cream
100 ml/3½ fl oz milk

1   Remove the heads and backbones from the anchovies. Leave to soak for 20 minutes, changing the water frequently. Dry well.

2   Peel the potatoes and slice thinly. Cut the onions into thin strips.

3   Melt half the butter in a frying pan, add the oil, and fry the onions over moderate heat for 4 minutes.

4   Butter an ovenproof dish. Add a layer of

potatoes, a layer of onions, and a thin layer of anchovies. Season lightly with salt and pepper.

5   Continue the layers until the ingredients are all used, finishing with potatoes. Cover the top with the remaining butter.

6   Gently heat the cream and milk in a small saucepan and pour over the potatoes and anchovies. Bake in a preheated oven at 220°C/425°F/ mark 7 for 30 minutes or until golden brown.

Suggested menu

Crab Venetian style
Jansson's temptation
Chestnut truffles

Suggested wines

Torgiano Bianco, Soave (Italy); Meursault (France); Californian Gewürztraminer (U.S.A.); Rhine Sylvaner (Germany).

Sea bream niçoise

Preparation: 40 minutes

1 1-kg/2¼-lb sea bream
salt and pepper
3 large ripe tomatoes
125 ml/4 fl oz oil
½ onion
bouquet garni (thyme, bay leaf, sage)
125 ml/4 fl oz white wine
12 anchovy fillets
12 black olives

1   Clean and scale the fish and cut off the fins. Wash and dry and sprinkle with salt and pepper.

2   Peel the tomatoes, remove seeds, and chop coarsely.

3   Pour half the oil into an ovenproof casserole and place the fish in whole.

4   Sprinkle with the remaining oil and add the chopped onion, tomatoes, and bouquet garni. Pour in the wine.

5   Bake in a preheated oven at 200°C/400°F/mark 6 for 20 minutes, basting occasionally with the liquid.

6   Wrap an anchovy fillet around each olive, secure with a cocktail stick and add to the casserole. Cook for a further 5 minutes. Discard the bouquet garni and cocktail sticks and transfer to a serving dish.

Suggested menu

Spaghetti with clams
Sea bream niçoise
Lemon tart

Suggested wines

Lugana, Pinot grigio dell'Alto Adige (Italy); Chablis (France); Californian Sauvignon Blanc (U.S.A.); Rhine Riesling (Germany).

Leghorn red mullet

Preparation: 1 hour

8 red mullet, total
  weight 800 g/1¾ lb
plain flour
8 tbsp oil
1 stick celery

2 cloves garlic
400 g/14 oz ripe
  tomatoes (or tinned)
salt
black pepper
1 tbsp chopped
  parsley

1   Clean, rinse, and dry the fish and coat lightly in flour.

2   Heat 5 tbsp oil until very hot and fry the fish over high heat for 3 minutes on each side. Drain and keep warm.

3   Finely chop the celery and garlic and fry gently in a large saucepan for 3 minutes in the remaining oil.

4   Add the peeled and chopped tomatoes, salt, and pepper and cook uncovered for 15 minutes.

5   Pass the tomato sauce through a vegetable mill or liquidize briefly.

6   Return the fish to the pan, cover with the tomato sauce, and reheat gently for 15 minutes.

7   Arrange the fish on a warm serving dish, cover with the sauce, and sprinkle with chopped parsley. Serve immediately.

Suggested menu

Spaghetti with tuna
Leghorn red mullet
Strawberries in Champagne

Suggested wines

Vernaccia di San Gimignano, Regaleali Bianco (Italy); Chablis (France); Californian Chardonnay (U.S.A.); Fumé Blanc (South Africa).

Portuguese salt cod

Preparation: 1 hour
(+ 2 days for soaking
the salt cod)

450 g/1 lb salt cod
450 g/1 lb potatoes
1 onion

175 ml/6 fl oz oil
salt
1 clove garlic
80 g/3 oz butter
4 eggs
2 tbsp parsley
black olives

1   Soak the salt cod in cold water for 2 days, changing the water frequently. Drain, remove the bones, and cut into 5-cm/2-in pieces.

2   Cut the potatoes into thin strips. Chop the onion.

3   Heat half the oil and fry the potatoes until golden brown. Drain on kitchen paper, sprinkle with salt, and keep warm.

4   Heat the remaining oil and fry the onion and crushed garlic for 1 minute before adding the salt cod. Cook for 8 minutes, turning frequently.

5   Melt the butter in another frying pan; add the eggs, and fry gently for 3 minutes. The eggs should still be soft.

6   Arrange the salt cod, French fries, and eggs on a serving dish, sprinkle with chopped parsley, and garnish with olives.

Suggested menu

Spaghetti with clams
Portuguese salt cod
Strawberries and bananas au citron

Suggested wines

Pinot dell'Oltrepò Pavese, Vernaccia di San Gimignano (Italy); Chassagne Montrachet (France); Californian Johannisberg Riesling (U.S.A.); Rhine Riesling (Germany).

Salt cod Vicenza style

Preparation: 2 hours
(+ 2 days for soaking
the salt cod)

800 g/1¾ lb salt cod
2 onions
1 clove garlic
2 anchovies

1 tbsp parsley
salt
pepper
225 ml/8 fl oz oil
50 g/2 oz grated
    Parmesan
500 ml/18 fl oz milk

Suggested menu

Crab Venetian style
Salt cod Vicenza style
Lemon soufflé

Suggested wines

Pinot Champenois del Trentino, Franciacorta
(Italy); Champagne (France); Californian Blanc
de Noirs (U.S.A.); Chardonnay (New Zealand).

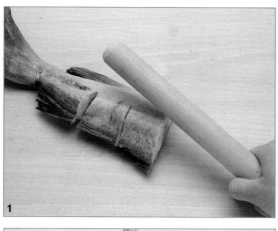

1 Beat the salt cod with a wooden rolling pin, then leave to soak in cold water for 2 days, changing the water frequently.

2 Cut the salt cod into strips 5 cm/2 in wide; open them out and remove the bones.

3 Skin each piece.

4 Finely chop the onions, garlic, anchovies, and parsley. Season with salt and pepper. Heat half the oil in a saucepan and fry the ingredients for 5 minutes before adding the Parmesan. Stir well.

5 Use the filling to sandwich the pieces of salt cod together.

6 Heat the remaining oil in a frying pan, add the salt cod topped with any remaining filling.

7 Heat for 2 minutes, then pour in the milk.

8 Cook very gently for 1½ hours, shaking the pan occasionally to prevent the salt cod from sticking. Serve with slices of fried polenta.

Florentine salt cod

Preparation: 50 minutes
(+ 2 days for soaking the
salt cod)

800 g/1¾ lb salt cod
plain flour

350 ml/12 fl oz oil
salt and pepper
450 g/1 lb ripe tomatoes
1 onion
1 sprig rosemary
1 clove garlic

Suggested menu

Sardines in 'saòr'
Florentine salt cod
Rhubarb soufflé

Suggested wines

Soave, Tocai del Collio (Italy); Pinot d'Alsace
(France); Californian Johannisberg Riesling
(U.S.A.); Riesling (Australia).

1   Soak the salt cod in cold water for 2 days, changing the water frequently. Drain, dry and coat lightly with flour.

2   Warm the oil in a saucepan; add the pieces of salt cod and fry gently for 20 minutes, spooning with the oil occasionally.

3   Remove the salt cod from the oil, drain on kitchen paper, and sprinkle with salt.

4   Place the roughly chopped tomatoes in a small saucepan with 1 tablespoon oil, sprinkle with salt, and cook for 10 minutes.

5   Pass the tomatoes through a fine strainer or liquidize.

6   Heat 2 tablespoons oil in a separate saucepan, add the finely chopped onion, salt, and a few tablespoons water. Fry until browned.

7   Add the salt cod and, after 2 minutes, the tomato sauce. Adjust the seasoning, add the rosemary, and cook for a further 3 minutes.

8   Finely chop the garlic and brown in a small saucepan for 2 minutes over very gentle heat in 3 tablespoons oil. Pour over the salt cod, sprinkle with pepper, and serve at once.

Brandade de morue

(Cream of salt cod)

Preparation: 1 hour
(+ 2 days for soaking
the salt cod)

800 g/1¾ lb salt cod
150 ml/5 fl oz oil

1 clove garlic
150 ml/5 fl oz milk
juice of ½ lemon
black pepper
single cream
parsley

1   Soak the salt cod in cold water for 2 days, changing the water frequently.

2   Cut the salt cod into large pieces, place in a large saucepan, and cover with cold water. Bring to the boil, lower the heat and simmer for 20 minutes.

3   Drain, remove the skin and bones, and flake or chop the salt cod. Heat half the oil in a saucepan and add the flaked salt cod. Cook gently for 5 minutes, stirring constantly.

4   Chop the garlic and heat the milk.

5   Add the garlic to the salt cod and gradually stir in the remaining oil and the milk, a tablespoon at a time. This step should be carried out slowly so that the mixture is perfectly smooth.

6   At the last minute, stir in the lemon juice and black pepper. Spoon the creamed salt cod on to heated individual plates and garnish with cream and parsley.

Suggested menu

Prawn risotto
Brandade de morue
Strawberries in Champagne

Suggested wines

Montecarlo Bianco, Pinot dell'Oltrepò Pavese (Italy); Pouilly-Fuissé (France); Californian Chardonnay (U.S.A.); Rhine Riesling (Germany).

Baked cod with horseradish sauce

Preparation: 50 minutes

800 g/1¾ lb cod fillets
salt and pepper
½ tbsp vinegar
50 g/2 oz butter

1 apple
25 g/1 oz fresh horseradish
200 ml/7 fl oz sour cream
½ tsp sugar
1 tbsp chopped parsley

1 Arrange the cod fillets in an ovenproof casserole, sprinkle evenly with salt, pepper, and vinegar.

2 Melt the butter and pour over the cod. Bake in a preheated oven at 200°C/400°F/mark 6 for 10 minutes.

3 Peel and grate the apple.

4 Mix together the grated apple, grated horseradish, sour cream, and sugar.

5 Pour the sour cream mixture over the fish. Turn the oven down slightly and bake for a further 10 minutes.

6 Serve the baked cod with boiled potatoes sprinkled with parsley.

Suggested menu

Sea date soup
Baked cod with horseradish sauce
Ladies' kisses

Suggested wines

Spumante Champenois dell'Oltrepò Pavese, Pinot Grigio dell'Alto Adige (Italy); Champagne (France); Californian Johannisberg Riesling (U.S.A.); Rhine Sylvaner (Germany).

Macaroni with fresh sardines and dill

Preparation: 1 hour
(+ 30 minutes for
soaking the sultanas)

2–3 tbsp sultanas
125 g/4 oz fresh dill
salt and pepper

350 g/12 oz fresh sardines
1 large onion
6 tbsp oil
3 tomatoes
25 g/1 oz pine nuts
4 anchovy fillets
250 g/9 oz macaroni

1   Soak the sultanas in warm water for 30 minutes. Trim and wash the dill, reserving the feathery green leaves. Cook the dill in plenty of salted water for 10 minutes. Drain well, reserving the water, and chop.

2   Clean and rinse the sardines; cut off the heads, open out flat, and pat dry with kitchen paper.

3   Fry the finely chopped onion in the oil for 5 minutes in a large frying pan. Add the seeded and chopped tomatoes, pine nuts, and drained sultanas.

4   Cook for a further 5 minutes, then add the sardines and chopped dill. Season with salt and pepper, cover, and simmer for 10 minutes.

5   Add the finely chopped anchovy fillets and cook for another 5 minutes.

6   Bring the reserved cooking water to the boil and cook the macaroni for 10 to 12 minutes or until *al dente*. Drain well and mix gently with the sardine, anchovy, and tomato mixture.

Suggested menu

Macaroni with fresh sardines and dill
Stewed baby octopus
Chilled orange soufflé

Suggested wines

Regaleali Bianco, Torbato (Italy); Graves Blanc (France); Californian Johannisberg Riesling (U.S.A.); Riesling (Australia).

Sardines in 'saòr'

Preparation: 1 hour
(+ 30 minutes for
soaking the sultanas
and 1 day for marinating
the sardines)

800 g/1¾ lb fresh
  sardines
plain flour

oil for deep frying
2 large onions
salt
125 ml/4 fl oz white
  wine vinegar
1–2 tbsp sultanas
25 g/1 oz pine nuts
1 tbsp candied peel
125 ml/4 fl oz sour cream

Suggested menu

Sardines in 'saòr'
Turbot with scampi sauce
Zabaglione

Suggested wines

Verdicchio dei Castelli di Jesi, Tocai del Collio
(Italy); Pinot d'Alsace (France); Californian
Chenin Blanc (U.S.A.); Sauvignon Blanc (South
Africa).

1   Remove the scales, clean the sardines, and rinse thoroughly.

2   Drain the sardines well and coat lightly with flour.

3   Fry the sardines in plenty of very hot oil.

4   When the sardines are golden brown and cooked, drain on kitchen paper.

5   Slice the onions finely, sprinkle with salt, and fry in 2 tbsp oil. Add 125 ml/ 4 fl oz water and cook for 10 minutes. Pour in half the vinegar and simmer for a few minutes.

6   Place the sardines in a shallow dish, pour over the remaining vinegar, and sprinkle with the soaked and drained sultanas, the pine nuts, and chopped candied peel.

7   Sprinkle with the onions and sour cream. Cover and leave to stand in a cool place—not in the refrigerator—for 24 hours before serving.

German sea bass

Preparation: 1 hour

1 800-g/1¾-lb sea
   bass
1 large onion
450 g/1 lb potatoes
salt

50 g/2 oz butter
1 tbsp oil
2 tsp German mustard
pepper
gherkins
4 eggs

1   Clean and fillet the sea
bass.

2   Chop the onion. Peel
and quarter the potatoes.

3   Cook the fish fillets for
8 minutes in boiling salted
water. Drain and keep
warm.

4   Boil the potatoes in
salted water for 20
minutes. Drain and mash
coarsely.

5   Melt the butter in a
frying pan, add the oil, and
heat. Fry the onion for

about 8 minutes. Stir in the
mustard and fry for
another minute.

6   Mix together the
potatoes and sea bass in a
bowl and season with salt
and pepper.

7   Arrange the fish and
potatoes on a heated
serving dish and pour over
the onion and cooking
juices.

8   Garnish with sliced
gherkins and serve with
fried eggs.

Suggested menu

Seafood soup
German sea bass
Wild strawberries and ice cream

Suggested wines

Sauvignon del Collio, Corvo di Salaparuta
(Italy); Pinot d'Alsace (France); Californian
Chardonnay (U.S.A.); Rhine Riesling
(Germany).

Fried sea bass in sweet and sour sauce

Preparation: 1 hour 10 minutes

1 spring onion
½ green pepper
1 1-kg/2¼-lb sea bass
salt
pepper

125 ml/4 fl oz oil
1 tbsp grated fresh ginger
125 ml/4 fl oz vinegar
1 tbsp dry sherry
2 tbsp sugar
25 g/1 oz cornflour
2 tbsp soy sauce

1   Finely slice the spring onion, including the green part. Cut the green pepper into thin strips, discarding the seeds.

2   Remove the scales from the sea bass, clean, rinse, and wipe dry. Sprinkle with salt and pepper.

3   Heat the oil in a frying pan and fry the fish over high heat for 3 minutes on each side. Lower the heat and cook for another 15 minutes. Drain, place on a serving dish, and keep warm.

4   Leave 1 tablespoon oil in the frying pan used for the sea bass. Add the spring onion and fresh ginger. Stir and fry for 1 minute.

5   Add the green pepper and cook for a further 3 minutes. Pour in the vinegar, sherry, sugar, the cornflour mixed with 50 ml/2 fl oz water, and soy sauce. Simmer gently, stirring until the sauce thickens. Pour over the fish and serve at once.

Suggested menu

Freshwater crayfish à la nage
Fried sea bass in sweet and sour sauce
Calvados sorbet

Suggested wines

Spumante Champenois del Trentino, Pinot dell'Oltrepò Pavese (Italy); Champagne (France); Californian Blanc de Blancs (U.S.A.); Pinot Riesling (Australia).

Baked stuffed sea bass

Preparation: 1 hour

½ onion
½ green pepper
1 large tomato
80 g/3 oz butter

1 1-kg/2¼-lb sea bass
1 tbsp chopped
  parsley
salt and pepper
125 ml/4 fl oz white wine
fresh dill

Suggested menu

Potted crab
Baked stuffed sea bass
Raspberries with zabaglione

Suggested wines

Montecarlo Bianco, Frascati (Italy); Moselle
Riesling (Germany); Californian
Gewürztraminer (U.S.A.); Chardonnay (South
Africa).

1 Finely chop the onion and pepper.

2 Peel the tomato, remove the seeds, and chop coarsely.

3 Melt half the butter in a frying pan and fry the onion, pepper, and tomato for 5 minutes.

4 Remove the scales from the sea bass. Slit open, then gut the fish. Rinse well under running water and wipe dry.

5 Stuff the fish with the onion, pepper, tomato, and chopped parsley. Season with salt and pepper.

6 Sew up the opening carefully with kitchen thread.

7 Place the fish in a buttered roasting tin. Pour over the wine and the remaining melted butter.

8 Bake in a preheated oven at 200°C/400°F/mark 6 for 20 minutes, basting frequently with the juices and sprinkling with chopped dill after 10 minutes.

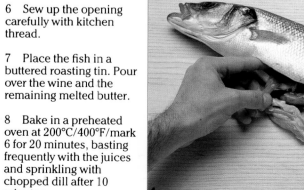

Baked sea bass with fennel

Preparation: 1 hour

1 1-kg/2¼-lb sea bass
6 sprigs fennel
salt and pepper
4 tbsp oil
125 ml/4 fl oz Pernod
   or Pastis

1   Remove the scales and gut the sea bass, leaving head and tail intact. Rinse and wipe dry.

2   Make diagonal cuts on both sides of the fish and insert sprigs of fennel.

3   Season with salt and pepper and brush with oil.

4   Place on a grill rack and bake in a preheated oven at 200°C/400°F/mark 6 for 20 minutes, turning halfway through cooking.

5   Place the fish on a preheated serving dish.

6   Heat the Pernod or Pastis in a small saucepan, pour over the fish, and flame.

Suggested menu

Chilled oyster soup
Baked sea bass with fennel
Pineapple Bavarian cream with puréed
   strawberries

Suggested wines

Sylvaner dell'Alto Adige, Lugana (Italy); Graves Blanc (France); Californian Chenin Blanc (U.S.A.); Moselle Riesling (Germany).

Conger eel Braganza style

Preparation: 1 hour

800 g/1¾ lb conger eel
125 ml/4 fl oz oil
1 small onion
1 bay leaf

1 tbsp vinegar
salt and pepper
4 slices day-old bread
3 egg yolks
1 tbsp chopped
   parsley

1   Wash and dry the eel and cut into four slices.

2   Heat the oil in a saucepan, add the chopped onion, and fry gently for 5 minutes.

3   Add the eel, bay leaf, vinegar, 250 ml/9 fl oz water, salt, and pepper. Bring to the boil and simmer for 10 minutes.

4   Arrange the slices of day-old bread on a heated serving dish and place the drained pieces of eel on top. Keep warm. Reserve the cooking liquid.

5   Beat together the egg yolks and parsley.

6   Stir the cooking juices gradually into the beaten egg yolks and parsley and heat gently until thickened. Pour the sauce over the eel and serve at once.

Suggested menu

Prawn cocktail
Conger eel Braganza style
Lemon soufflé

Suggested wines

Regaleali Bianco, Torgiano Bianco (Italy); Meursault (France); Californian Johannisberg Riesling (U.S.A.); Chardonnay (Australia).

Stuffed hake

Preparation: 1 hour

1 1.2-kg/2¾-lb hake
3 hard-boiled eggs
50 g/2 oz ham
10 black olives

½ red pepper
8 tbsp oil
1 tbsp breadcrumbs
1 bay leaf
1 large ripe tomato
salt and black pepper

Suggested menu

Crab Venetian style
Stuffed hake
Fruit salad in gin

Suggested wines

Torbato, Regaleali Bianco (Italy); Bordeaux
Blanc (France); Californian Sauvignon Blanc
(U.S.A.); Rhine Riesling (South Africa).

1 Remove the scales, gut, and rinse the hake.

2 Prepare the stuffing first. Chop the hard-boiled eggs.

3 Coarsely chop the ham.

4 Stone the olives and chop into small pieces, together with the red pepper.

5 Mix the ingredients together, adding 2 tablespoons oil and the breadcrumbs; spoon the stuffing inside the fish.

6 Sew up the cavity of the fish with kitchen thread. Pour the remaining oil into an ovenproof dish. Place the fish inside and sprinkle with the crumbled bay leaf.

7 Spoon the coarsely chopped tomato over the fish. Season with salt and pepper and bake in a preheated oven at 180°C/350°F/mark 4 for 30 minutes, basting occasionally with the cooking juices or with a few tablespoons water.

Sea bream with olives

Preparation: 40 minutes

1 1.2-kg/2¾-lb sea bream
6 tbsp oil

24 black olives
salt and pepper
200 ml/7 fl oz white wine
4 sprigs rosemary

1 Remove the scales; gut, and rinse the sea bream.

2 Pour the oil into a large frying pan and fry the fish gently for 3 minutes on each side.

3 Add the stoned olives, season with salt, and pour in the wine. Cook for a further 15 minutes.

4 Add the sprigs of rosemary, sprinkle generously with pepper, and cook for another 5 minutes. Serve immediately.

Suggested menu

Prawn risotto
Sea bream with olives
Raspberries with zabaglione

Suggested wines

Vernaccia di San Gimignano, Verdicchio dei Castelli di Jesi (Italy); Montrachet (France); Californian Gewürztraminer (U.S.A.); Rhine Riesling (South Africa).

John Dory with vegetables

Preparation: 45 minutes

1 1-kg/2¼-lb John Dory (turbot or sole may be substituted)
plain flour
8 tbsp oil
salt
4 artichokes
sprig rosemary
juice of ½ lemon
200 ml/7 fl oz white wine
1 tbsp chopped parsley
black pepper
25 g/1 oz butter

1   Clean and rinse the fish and cut into four. Wipe dry and coat lightly with flour.

2   Heat the oil in a large frying pan and, when hot, place the pieces of fish in side by side.

3   Fry for 3 minutes on each side, then sprinkle with salt.

4   Trim the artichokes, discarding the tough outer leaves. Slice finely and add to the pan together with the rosemary. Season with salt.

5   Pour in the lemon juice, add the wine, and cook for about 15 minutes.

6   Sprinkle with the finely chopped parsley and black pepper and cook, uncovered, for 3 minutes.

7   Arrange the artichokes on a heated serving dish and place the fish on top.

8   Make a beurre manié by mixing together 1 tablespoon flour with the butter; stir into the sauce to thicken, then pour over the fish.

Suggested menu

Spaghetti with spiny lobster
John Dory with vegetables
Passion fruit sorbet

Suggested wines

Riesling dell'Oltrepò Pavese, Tocai del Collio (Italy); Pouilly-Fuissé (France); Californian Sauvignon Blanc (U.S.A.); Chardonnay (South Africa).

81

Turbot with scampi sauce

Preparation: 1 hour

3 Dublin Bay prawns
½ tbsp plain flour
salt
80 g/3 oz butter
pinch mace

Cayenne pepper
1 1.2-kg/2¾-lb turbot
200 ml/7 fl oz milk
½ lemon
pepper
1 tbsp chopped
  parsley

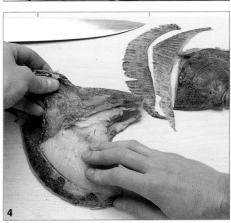

1　Boil the Dublin Bay prawns for 3 minutes in 5 cm/2 in of water. Shell them, return the shells to the water, and cook for a further 15 minutes. Strain the fumet and reduce by boiling vigorously.

2　Mix the flour with 125 ml/4 fl oz of the fumet and add a pinch of salt. Add the butter in pieces and cook, stirring constantly, for 3 minutes.

3　Add the meat from the Dublin Bay prawns, cut into pieces, a pinch of mace, and Cayenne pepper. Stir for 1 minute until the sauce thickens.

4　Clean the turbot: cut off the head and fins and remove the skin.

5　Cover with 200 ml/ 7 fl oz water and the milk, then add the lemon juice. Season with salt and pepper and cook for about 15 minutes.

6　Drain the turbot, place on a warm serving dish, and sprinkle with chopped parsley. Serve with boiled potatoes and carrots and serve the scampi sauce separately in a sauce boat.

Suggested menu

Soused herrings
Turbot with scampi sauce
Fruit salad in gin

Suggested wines

Spumante Champenois del Trentino, Pinot Bianco di Franciacorta (Italy); Champagne (France); Chenin Blanc (South Africa); Moselle Riesling (Germany).

Grilled or barbecued turbot

1 1.2-kg/2¾-lb turbot
1 tbsp sea salt
2 cloves garlic
3 tbsp oil
parsley
1 lemon

Serve with: Béarnaise
sauce (page 182)

1   Clean the turbot:
remove entrails and skin
but leave head intact.
Rinse and dry.

2   Prepare the brine: in a
shallow roasting pan
gently heat 2 ladles of
water, the sea salt, and
crushed garlic.

3   Brush the turbot on
both sides with oil.

4   Place the fish on a grill
rack in a hot oven (200°C/
400°F/mark 6) or on a
barbecue grill.

5   Turn the fish every 4
minutes, dipping it in the
brine each time. Repeat 4
times or until tender.

6   Serve with Béarnaise
sauce and garnish with
parsley and lemon.

Suggested menu

Seafood salad
Grilled or barbecued turbot
Pineapple ice cream

Suggested wines

Torbato, Tocai del Collio (Italy); Sancerre
(France); Californian Chenin Blanc (U.S.A.);
Chardonnay (South Africa).

Crustaceans

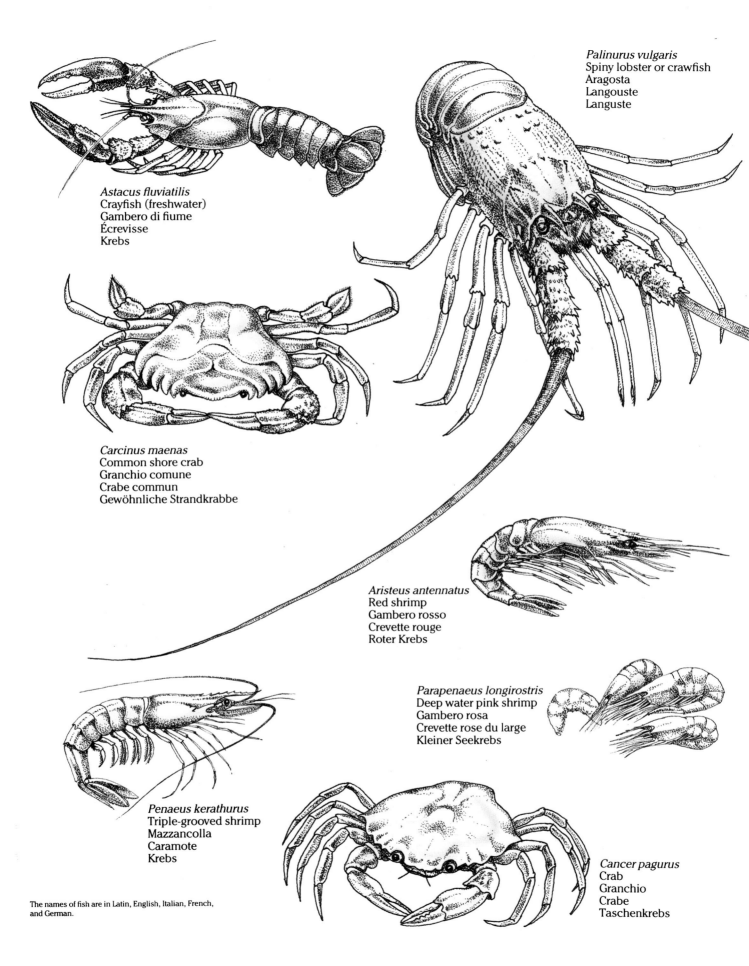

Astacus fluviatilis
Crayfish (freshwater)
Gambero di fiume
Écrevisse
Krebs

Palinurus vulgaris
Spiny lobster or crawfish
Aragosta
Langouste
Languste

Carcinus maenas
Common shore crab
Granchio comune
Crabe commun
Gewöhnliche Strandkrabbe

Aristeus antennatus
Red shrimp
Gambero rosso
Crevette rouge
Roter Krebs

Parapenaeus longirostris
Deep water pink shrimp
Gambero rosa
Crevette rose du large
Kleiner Seekrebs

Penaeus kerathurus
Triple-grooved shrimp
Mazzancolla
Caramote
Krebs

Cancer pagurus
Crab
Granchio
Crabe
Taschenkrebs

The names of fish are in Latin, English, Italian, French, and German.

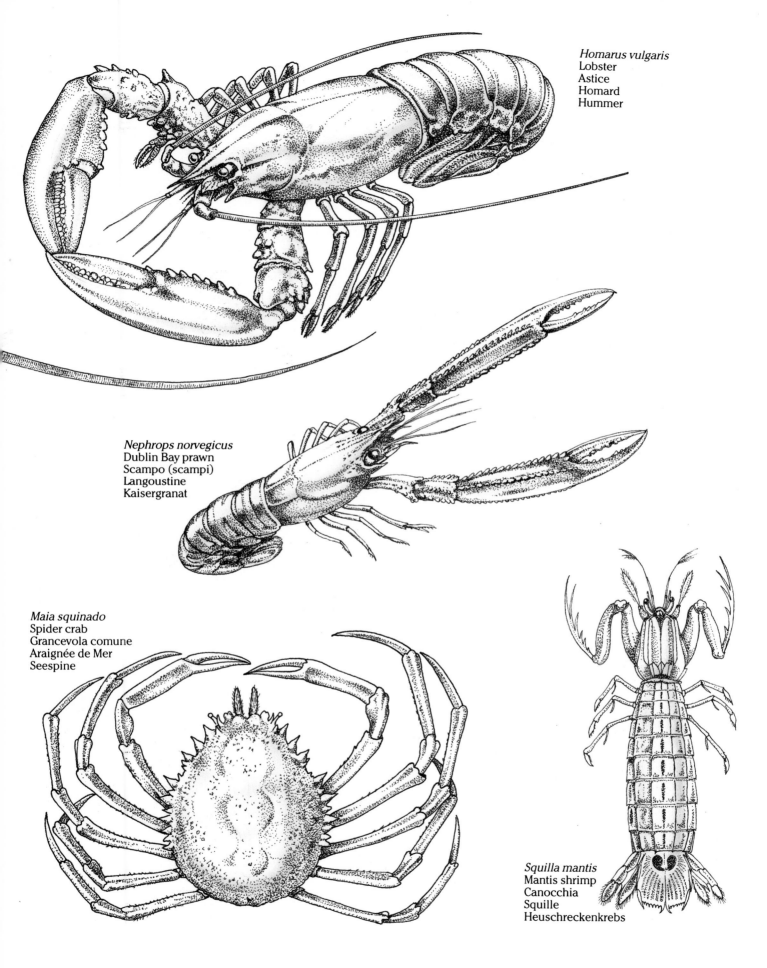

Homarus vulgaris
Lobster
Astice
Homard
Hummer

Nephrops norvegicus
Dublin Bay prawn
Scampo (scampi)
Langoustine
Kaisergranat

Maia squinado
Spider crab
Grancevola comune
Araignée de Mer
Seespine

Squilla mantis
Mantis shrimp
Canocchia
Squille
Heuschreckenkrebs

Spaghetti with spiny lobster

Preparation: 1 hour

1 450-g/1-lb lobster
salt and pepper
½ onion

6 tbsp oil
2 ripe tomatoes
1 sprig rosemary
275 g/10 oz spaghetti

Suggested menu

Spaghetti with spiny lobster
Sea bass with orange sauce
Flambéed apricots

Suggested wines

Torbato, Vernaccia di San Gimignano (Italy);
Chassagne Montrachet (France); Californian
Johannisberg Riesling (U.S.A.); Sauvignon
Blanc (South Africa).

1   Tie the spiny lobster with string and plunge into a large pan of boiling salted water. Cook for 8 minutes.

2   Drain and leave to cool. Break off the tail and cut in half lengthwise using a sharp knife.

3   Remove the meat from the tail and cut into chunks.

4   Finely chop the onion and fry gently in 4 tablespoons oil in a large frying pan.

5   Add the peeled and roughly chopped tomatoes and a pinch of salt and cook for 5 minutes.

6   Add the pieces of lobster and rosemary and cook for another 3 minutes.

7   Cook the spaghetti in boiling salted water for 8 minutes or until *al dente*.

8   Drain the spaghetti, pour the remaining oil over it, and add to the sauce. Mix well for 2 minutes. Season with salt and pepper and serve immediately.

Spiny lobster Algerian style

Preparation: 1 hour

2 450-g/1-lb spiny
  lobsters
2 onions
6 tbsp oil

1 tsp mustard
1 tsp white wine
  vinegar
salt and pepper
2 medium tomatoes

Suggested menu

Clam soup
Spiny lobster Algerian style
Pineapple Bavarian cream with puréed
  strawberries

Suggested wines

Sauvignon del Collio, Torbato (Italy); Sancerre
(France); Californian Chenin Blanc (U.S.A.);
Fumé Blanc (South Africa).

1   Tie the spiny lobsters with string, plunge them into boiling salted water, and cook for 10 minutes.

2   Finely slice the onions and leave to soak in a cup of salted water for 10 minutes.

3   When the lobsters have cooled cut the tails in half.

4   Using a teaspoon carefully remove the creamy substance from the head and place in a bowl.

5   Add to it 5 tablespoons oil, the mustard, vinegar, salt and pepper, and stir vigorously.

6   Remove the meat from the tail and cut into slices.

7   Drain the onions, pour over the remaining oil, and chop the tomatoes into small pieces. Sprinkle with salt.

8   Arrange a layer of onion on each plate and place the slices of lobster on top. Pour over the sauce and sprinkle with the pieces of tomato.

Spiny lobster Catalan style

Preparation: 1 hour

2 450-g/1-lb spiny
  lobsters
salt and pepper
1 small onion
2 green peppers
4 tomatoes

200 ml/7 fl oz oil
1 tbsp chopped
  parsley
350 ml/12 fl oz dry
  white wine
1 tsp Cayenne pepper
¼ tsp saffron powder
2 tbsp Cognac

Suggested menu

Prawn cocktail
Spiny lobster Catalan style
Lemon tart

Suggested wines

Spumante Champenois dell'Oltrepò Pavese,
Torgiano (Italy); Montrachet (France);
Californian Chardonnay (U.S.A.); Sauvignon
Blanc (South Africa).

1 Tie the spiny lobsters with string and plunge into a large pan of boiling salted water. Cook for 8 minutes. Drain and leave to cool. Remove the meat from the tail and cut into chunks.

2 Finely chop the onion. Remove the seeds from the green peppers and cut into strips. Peel the tomatoes, discard seeds, and chop coarsely.

3 Heat the oil in a frying pan and fry the chunks of lobster over fairly high heat for a few minutes. Season with salt and pepper. Drain and keep warm.

4 Brown the onion in the same oil, then add the tomatoes and green peppers.

5 After 5 minutes add the parsley, white wine, Cayenne pepper, saffron and lobster. Cover and simmer for 10 minutes.

6 Remove the pieces of lobster and place on a warmed serving dish.

7 Reduce the sauce by boiling vigorously for 1 minute. Pour in the Cognac and flame.

8 Arrange the peppers around the lobster, pour over the sauce, and serve.

Lobster Thermidor

Preparation: 1½ hours

2 cooked lobsters,
  total weight 1.2 kg/2¾ lb
6 tbsp oil
salt and pepper
1–2 shallots
125 g/4 oz butter
125 ml/4 fl oz white wine

1 tsp tarragon
1 tsp chervil
50 g/2 oz plain flour
250 ml/9 fl oz fumet (page 181)
250 ml/9 fl oz milk
100 ml/3½ fl oz cream
2 egg yolks
25 g /1 oz grated
  Parmesan cheese

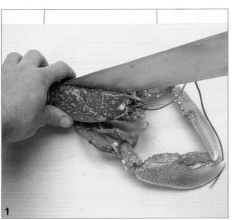

1 Cut the lobsters in half lengthwise. Extract and reserve the coral and liver. Brush both halves with oil and sprinkle with salt and pepper. Place the lobsters in a baking dish in a preheated oven (200°C/400°F/mark 6) for 15 minutes, brushing occasionally with oil.

2 Break off the head and remove the meat from the tails. Break the claws and extract the meat. Reserve the shells. Push the coral and liver through a sieve.

3 Melt 25 g/1 oz butter in a frying pan and briefly fry the chopped shallots. Add the wine, tarragon, and chervil. Lower the heat and simmer for a few minutes.

4 Melt 50 g/2 oz butter in a saucepan, stir in the flour, and cook for 1 minute. Gradually stir in the hot fumet and milk. Bring to the boil and simmer for 2 minutes.

5 Mix together the cream, egg yolks and sieved coral and liver. Stir into the white sauce and cook for 2 minutes. Stir in the fried shallot and herb mixture. Season with salt and pepper and add the lobster meat.

6 Pour the mixture into the shells. Sprinkle with Parmesan, pour over the remaining melted butter, and brown in a hot oven for 5 minutes.

Suggested menu

Freshwater crayfish à la nage
Lobster Thermidor
Ladies' kisses

Suggested wines

Pinot Bianco del Collio, Terlano dell'Alto Adige (Italy); Pouilly-Fuissé (France); Californian Chenin Blanc (U.S.A.); Fumé Blanc (South Africa).

Lobster Newburg

Preparation: 40 minutes

1 1-kg/2¼-lb lobster
  or spiny lobster
salt
50 g/2 oz butter
125 ml/4 fl oz Madeira
  or Marsala wine

500 ml/18 fl oz cream
5 egg yolks
pinch Cayenne
  pepper
pepper
225 g/8 oz long-grain
  rice
1 tbsp chopped
  parsley

1   Tie the lobster with string and cook in a large pan of boiling salted water for about 15 minutes.

2   Leave to cool slightly, then remove the meat from the tail and cut into chunks.

3   Melt the butter in a frying pan and heat the pieces of lobster for 2 minutes.

4   Pour in the Madeira and 350 ml/12 fl oz cream. Bring to the boil, lower the heat, and simmer for 2 minutes.

5   Mix the egg yolks with the remaining cream and a few tablespoons of the Madeira sauce.

6   Add the Madeira mixture to the frying pan, stirring constantly. Heat gently until the sauce thickens but do not allow to boil.

7   Season with a pinch of Cayenne pepper, salt and black pepper.

8   Cook for a further 2 to 3 minutes. Serve on a bed of steamed rice and sprinkle with chopped parsley.

Suggested menu

Prawn pilaf
Lobster Newburg
Flambéed pineapple

Suggested wines

Ribolla dei Colli Orientali del Friuli, Pinot dell'Oltrepò Pavese (Italy); Sancerre (France); Californian Pinot Blanc (U.S.A.); Rhine Riesling (Germany).

Lobster à l'américaine

Preparation: 1 hour

2 450-g/1-lb cooked
   lobsters
salt and pepper
100 ml/3½ fl oz oil
½ onion, 2 shallots
1 clove garlic
125 ml/4 fl oz Cognac

250 ml/9 fl oz white wine
4 ripe tomatoes
200 ml/7 fl oz fumet
   (page 181)
pinch Cayenne pepper
1 tbsp tomato purée
2 tbsp parsley
1 tbsp tarragon
25 g/1 oz butter

1   Cut the lobsters in half lengthwise, removing and reserving the coral and liver, and cut each half tail into three and the head into two. Remove the claws. Season with salt and pepper. Heat the oil in a frying pan, add the lobster pieces, including the claws, and fry over high heat for 4 minutes.

2   Remove the pieces of lobster and add the chopped onion, shallots, and garlic. Fry gently for 8 minutes, return the lobster to the pan, pour over the Cognac and flame. Stir in the wine, chopped tomatoes, fumet, and Cayenne pepper. Cover and simmer for 5 minutes.

3   Remove the meat from the claws and tails and keep warm. Pound the shells and heads and return to the sauce. Add the tomato purée and cook for 5 minutes. Sieve the sauce and reduce over high heat. Stir in the coral and liver, the parsley and tarragon, and the pieces of lobster. Simmer for 1 minute, stir in the butter and heat for a further minute before serving.

Suggested menu

Prawn pilaf
Lobster à l'américaine
Aniseed and almond biscuits

Suggested wines

Vernaccia di San Gimignano, Regaleali Bianco (Italy); Montrachet (France); Californian Sauvignon Blanc (U.S.A.); Rhine Sylvaner (Germany).

Crab Venetian style

Preparation: 45 minutes

4 spider crabs, total
    weight 1 kg/2¼ lb
salt and pepper
bunch parsley
4 tbsp oil
1 lemon

Suggested menu

Crab Venetian style
Fillets of sole à la normande
Raspberry Bavarian cream

Suggested wines

Pinot grigio dell'Alto Adige, Soave (Italy);
Muscadet (France); Californian Pinot Blanc
(U.S.A.); Chardonnay (Australia).

1   Plunge the crabs into boiling salted water and cook for 6 minutes.

2   Drain the crabs and leave to cool; pull away the legs and crack open with the aid of a nutcracker. Remove the flesh and chop finely.

3   Turn the crab over and pull the body away from the shell. Using a teaspoon, scrape out the eggs and set aside.

4   Remove all the meat (discard the grey stomach sac and 'dead men's fingers') from the shell.

5   Finely chop the meat and add to the chopped flesh from the legs. Reserve the shells.

6   Finely chop the parsley.

7   Spoon the chopped meat back into the reserved shells and place a spoonful of the eggs in the centre of each. Sprinkle with chopped parsley and season with oil, lemon juice, salt and pepper.

Potted crab

Preparation: 1 hour

1 1.2-kg/2¾-lb crab
salt
¾ teaspoon Cayenne
  pepper
¼ teaspoon nutmeg
pinch mace
1 lemon
225 g/8 oz butter
80 g/3 oz clarified
  butter (page 181)

Suggested menu

Potted crab
Eel Venetian style
Lemon soufflé

Suggested wines

Pinot Bianco del Collio, Montecarlo Bianco
(Italy); Gewürztraminer d'Alsace (France);
Californian Chenin Blanc (U.S.A.); Sauvignon
Blanc (South Africa).

1   Plunge the crab into boiling salted water and cook for 20 minutes.

2   Break off the claws and legs. Pull off and discard the grey feathery gills ('dead men's fingers') and the grey stomach sac. Spoon out the meat and separate the white from the creamier, darker part. Crack the claws and extract the meat.

3   Place the meat in two separate bowls. Season with salt, Cayenne pepper, nutmeg, mace, and lemon juice.

4   Spoon into ramekins in alternate layers of light and dark meat.

5   Melt the butter and divide equally between the ramekins.

6   Place the ramekins in a *bain-marie*; bake in a preheated oven at 170°C/325°F/mark 3 for 15 minutes.

7   Allow to cool before turning out.

8   Pour a little extra melted butter over each one if desired and serve with toasted bread. Alternatively, pour the clarified butter into the ramekins to form a seal and chill in the refrigerator.

Maryland crab rissoles

Preparation: 1 hour 20 minutes (+ 1 hour for refrigeration)

1 1-kg/2¼-lb crab
125 g/4 oz onions
salt and pepper
225 ml/8 fl oz oil
2 eggs

4 tbsp mayonnaise
2 tbsp mustard
2 drops Tabasco
2 tbsp parsley
100 g/3½ oz fine breadcrumbs

Serve with: tartare sauce (page 182)

Suggested menu

Maryland crab rissoles
Grilled or barbecued turbot
Raspberries with zabaglione

Suggested wines

Vernaccia di San Gimignano, Terlano dell'Alto Adige (Italy); Chassagne Montrachet (France); Californian Johannisberg Riesling (U.S.A.); Chenin Blanc (South Africa).

1   Plunge the crabs into boiling salted water and cook for 20 minutes or until they turn bright red. Discard the grey feathery gills and stomach sac. Extract the meat from the shell as well as from the legs and claws.

2   Chop the meat.

3   Chop the onions and fry for 4 minutes in a few tablespoons oil.

4   Beat the eggs and work in the mayonnaise, mustard, Tabasco, and salt and pepper.

5   In another bowl mix together the crabmeat, chopped parsley, 80 g/3 oz breadcumbs, the onions, and the egg mixture.

6   Shape the mixture into rissoles. Cover and refrigerate for 1 hour.

7   Heat the oil in a frying pan; dip the rissoles in the remaining breadcrumbs and fry in the hot oil for about 5 minutes or until golden brown, turning once.

8   Drain on kitchen paper and serve with tartare sauce.

Crab Louis

Preparation: 1 hour

1 1.2-kg/2¾-lb crab
salt
1 lettuce
2 tomatoes
2 hard-boiled eggs
1 small avocado
150 ml/5 fl oz mayonnaise

3 tbsp chopped onion
4 tbsp chilli sauce
1 tbsp Worcestershire
   sauce
Cayenne pepper
2 tbsp parsley
1 tbsp lemon juice
125 ml/4 fl oz
   whipped cream

1 Plunge the crab into boiling salted water and cook for 20 minutes until it turns bright red. Allow to cool slightly before extracting the meat from the body, claws, and legs.

2 Cut the lettuce into strips, rinse and drain. Arrange on a serving dish with the crabmeat on top.

3 Cut the tomatoes, eggs, and avocado into wedges and arrange around the crabmeat.

4 In a bowl blend together the mayonnaise, onions, chilli sauce, Worcestershire sauce, Cayenne pepper, chopped parsley, and lemon juice.

5 Fold in the whipped cream.

6 Spoon the sauce over the crabmeat and serve.

Suggested menu

Prawn risotto
Crab Louis
Chestnut truffles

Suggested wines

Corvo di Salaparuta, Torgiano Bianco (Italy); Bourgogne Blanc (France); Californian Pinot Blanc (U.S.A.); Moselle Riesling (Germany).

Deep-fried soft-shell crabs

Preparation: 2½ hours

800 g/1¾ lb live soft-shell crabs

2 eggs
salt
plain flour
oil for deep frying

1   Rinse the crabs and drain well.

2   Beat the eggs in a large bowl and season with salt.

3   Pour in the crabs and leave for 2 hours, during which time they will absorb a good deal of the egg and die. Remove from the bowl and dip in the flour.

4   Heat plenty of oil in a large frying pan and when hot add the crabs, a few at a time.

5   Fry briefly until crisp and golden brown. Drain on kitchen paper, sprinkle with salt, and serve at once.

Suggested menu

Deep-fried soft-shell crabs
Sea bass with orange sauce
Flambéed pineapple

Suggested wines

Pinot Bianco del Collio, Torbato (Italy); Muscadet (France); Californian Pinot Blanc (U.S.A.); Chenin Blanc (South Africa).

Scampi cocktail

Preparation: 30 minutes (+1 hour for refrigeration)

20 scampi (Dublin Bay prawns)
salt
200 ml/7 fl oz mayonnaise

1½ tbsp tomato ketchup
½ tsp Worcestershire sauce
2 tsp Cognac
1 lettuce
parsley
1 lemon

1.   Cook the scampi for 5 minutes in boiling salted water. Drain, leave to cool slightly, then shell.

2   Mix together the mayonnaise, ketchup, Worcestershire sauce, and Cognac.

3   Wash and dry the lettuce and finely shred the white part.

4   Mix the scampi with the sauce, reserving a few for the garnish.

5   Distribute the lettuce between 4 stemmed glasses, lining each with a whole outer leaf.

6   Spoon the scampi cocktail into each glass and garnish with a slice of lemon and a little parsley. Refrigerate for 1 hour before serving.

Suggested menu

Scampi cocktail
Sole with aniseed sauce
Passion fruit sorbet

Suggested wines

Gavi, Corvo di Salaparuta (Italy); Pouilly-Fuissé (France); Californian Chenin Blanc (U.S.A.); Fumé Blanc (South Africa).

Scampi in tomato and white wine sauce

Preparation: 30 minutes

20 scampi (Dublin Bay prawns)
4 tbsp oil
2 cloves garlic

salt and black pepper
350 g/12 oz tomatoes
200 ml/7 fl oz white wine
1 tbsp chopped parsley

Suggested menu

Anchovies with rice
Scampi in tomato and white wine sauce
Wild strawberries and ice cream

Suggested wines

Spumante Champenois del Trentino, Tocai del Collio (Italy); Champagne (France); Californian Sauvignon Blanc (U.S.A.); Riesling (Australia).

1   Rinse the scampi and with a sharp knife cut each one in half down the back.

2   Heat the oil in a large frying pan.

3   Coarsely chop the garlic and fry gently in the oil for 2 minutes.

4   Remove the garlic with a slotted spoon.

5   Place the scampi side by side on their backs in the flavoured oil.

6   Season with salt and plenty of freshly ground black pepper, then spoon over the coarsely chopped tomatoes. Cook for 2 minutes.

7   Pour in the white wine, cover, and simmer for 10 minutes. Sprinkle the scampi with chopped parsley and continue cooking uncovered for a further 2 minutes. Season with more black pepper and serve at once.

Curried jumbo prawns

Preparation: 1 hour
10 minutes

1 kg/2¼ lb jumbo
  prawns
salt
½ onion
1 tomato
1 clove garlic

6 tbsp oil
4 tbsp natural yogurt
½ tsp ginger
½ chilli pepper
1 tsp turmeric
½ tsp cumin
1 tbsp wine vinegar
½ tsp sugar
200 g/7 oz rice

1   Blanch the prawns in boiling salted water for 3 minutes and then remove the shells.

2   Chop the onion. Blanch and peel the tomato and remove the seeds.

3   In a blender or food processor mix together all the ingredients, with the exception of the onion and prawns, until the sauce is well blended.

4   Heat the oil in a frying pan and cook the prawns for 5 minutes. Remove

with a slotted spoon and drain.

5   Fry the onion until tender in the same pan in the remaining oil for 5 minutes.

6   Add the sauce from the blender to the saucepan and bring to the boil.

7   Lower the heat and simmer gently for 8 minutes, stirring occasionally, until the sauce has reduced slightly.

8   Add the prawns and cook for 3 minutes. Serve

on a bed of steamed rice and garnish with chopped parsley.

Suggested menu

Soused herrings
Curried jumbo prawns
Chilled orange soufflé

Suggested wines

Spumante Champenois dell'Oltrepò Pavese, Pinot Bianco del Collio (Italy); Champagne (France); Californian Sauvignon Blanc (U.S.A.); Chenin Blanc (South Africa).

Freshwater crayfish à la nage

Preparation: 1 hour

1 carrot
1 stick celery
½ onion
3 shallots
1 bay leaf
small piece chilli
   pepper

500 ml/18 fl oz white
   wine
1 tsp thyme
1 tsp black peppercorns
pinch Cayenne
   pepper
½ tsp aniseed
salt
24 freshwater crayfish

1   Finely slice the carrot, celery, onion, and shallots.

2   Place in a saucepan with 1 litre/1¾ pints water, the bay leaf, chilli pepper, wine, thyme, peppercorns, aniseed, and salt.

3   Bring to the boil, lower the heat, and simmer for 20 minutes. The *court-bouillon* will reduce considerably.

4   Wash the crayfish and use a sharp knife to remove the black intestine running down the middle of the tail.

5   Place the crayfish in the *court-bouillon*. Cover and simmer over moderate heat for 12 minutes or until the crayfish turn red.

6   Remove the crayfish, shell them, and keep warm. Pour the *court-bouillon* through a sieve.

7   Serve the crayfish in soup bowls with a little of the *court-bouillon*.

Suggested menu

Freshwater crayfish à la nage
Potted crab
Sablés

Suggested wines

Lugana, Trebbiano di Romagna (Italy);
Bordeaux Blanc (France); Californian Chenin Blanc (U.S.A.); Chardonnay (New Zealand).

Prawn risotto

Preparation: 1 hour

450 g/1 lb prawns
1 carrot
1 stick celery
salt, and pepper
½ onion

50 g/2 oz butter
2 tbsp oil
275 g/10 oz risotto
rice (arborio)
100 ml/3½ fl oz white wine
1 tbsp chopped
parsley

Suggested menu

Prawn risotto
Sea bass with 'tarator' sauce
Passion fruit sorbet

Suggested wines

Pinot Bianco del Collio, Regaleali Bianco (Italy);
Bourgogne Blanc (France); Californian Fumé
Blanc (U.S.A.); Chenin Blanc (New Zealand).

1   Peel the prawns.

2   Boil the heads and tails for 5 minutes in 5 ladles of water with the sliced carrot, celery, and a pinch of salt.

3   Crush the heads with a wooden spoon and pour the stock through a sieve.

4   Finely chop the onion. Melt half the butter in a risotto pan and cook the onion, adding 125 ml/ 4 fl oz water and a pinch of salt.

5   Melt the remaining butter in a frying pan, add the oil and prawns; sprinkle with salt and cook gently for 5 minutes.

6   When the onion is transparent, not brown, add the rice and the wine and stir over high heat for 2 minutes.

7   Once the rice is evenly coated, add the stock and cook over moderate heat, without stirring, until the rice is almost tender. Just before turning off the heat, add the prawns and sprinkle with pepper. The risotto should be very moist.

8   Turn off the heat, add a little extra butter and the chopped parsley and mix well with a wooden spoon. Cover and leave to stand for at least 2 minutes before serving.

Prawn cocktail

Preparation: 30 minutes (+ 40 minutes for refrigeration)

800 g/1¾ lb prawns
salt
125 ml/4 fl oz chilli sauce

125 ml/4 fl oz tomato ketchup
½ tsp grated horseradish
2 tsp lemon juice
1 lettuce
parsley
1 lemon

1   Place the prawns in a saucepan of boiling salted water and cook for 3 minutes.

2   Drain and shell the prawns and place in the refrigerator.

3   Mix together the chilli sauce, ketchup, horseradish, and lemon juice and chill in the refrigerator.

4   Finely shred half the lettuce.

5   Line four glass dishes with lettuce leaves and place the shredded lettuce in the bottom. Arrange the prawns on top.

6   Cover the prawns evenly with the sauce.

7   Garnish each glass with parsley and lemon slices and chill in the refrigerator before serving.

Suggested menu

Prawn cocktail
Eel stew
Almond squares

Suggested wines

Pinot Bianco del Collio, Lugana (Italy); Chablis (France); Californian Chenin Blanc (U.S.A.); Moselle Riesling (Germany).

Prawns à la créole

Preparation: 40 minutes

800 g/1¾ lb cooked prawns
2 small onions
1 stick celery
½ green pepper
1 clove garlic
325 g/12 oz ripe tomatoes
150 g/5 oz rice
1½ tbsp oil
50 g/2 oz butter
½ bay leaf
pinch thyme
1 tsp paprika
2 drops Tabasco
salt

1   Shell and rinse the prawns.

2   Chop the onions and celery. Dice the green pepper and chop the garlic. Remove the seeds from the tomatoes and chop.

3   Steam the rice for 15 minutes.

4   Heat the oil and butter in a frying pan. Add the onion, celery and pepper and fry for 5 minutes. Add the garlic and cook for 1 minute.

5   Add the bay leaf, thyme, paprika, Tabasco, and tomatoes. Season with salt.

6   Bring to the boil, lower the heat, and simmer for 15 minutes.

7   Stir in the prawns and cook for another 4 minutes. Serve with the steamed rice.

Suggested menu

Prawns à la créole
Sea bream with olives
Zabaglione

Suggested wines

Vermentino, Frascati (Italy); Montrachet (France); Californian Johannisberg Riesling (U.S.A.); Rhine Riesling (Germany).

Prawn pilaf

Preparation: 30 minutes

80 g/3 oz butter
250 g/9 oz long-grain rice
1 vegetable stock cube

salt and pepper
1 bay leaf
175 g/6 oz peeled prawns
1 tbsp chopped parsley

1 Melt half the butter in a saucepan and add the rice. Stir well over high heat for 2 minutes.

2 Cover with plenty of boiling water, add the chopped vegetable stock cube, ½ teaspoon salt, and the bay leaf. Remove the bay leaf after 5 minutes. Cover and cook, without stirring, until the rice is tender (15 to 20 minutes, depending on the quality of the rice).

3 Rinse and drain the prawns. Melt the remaining butter in a frying pan and sauté the prawns for 5 minutes, sprinkling with salt.

4 When the rice is cooked, remove from the heat, stir in the prawns, pepper, and chopped parsley and mix thoroughly. Turn on to a heated serving dish and place a few prawns on top.

Suggested menu

Prawn pilaf
Anguilles au vert
Almond and aniseed biscuits

Suggested wines

Pinot Bianco di Franciacorta, Riesling dell'Oltrepò Pavese (Italy); Muscadet (France); Californian Chenin Blanc (U.S.A.); Fumé Blanc (South Africa).

Freshwater fish

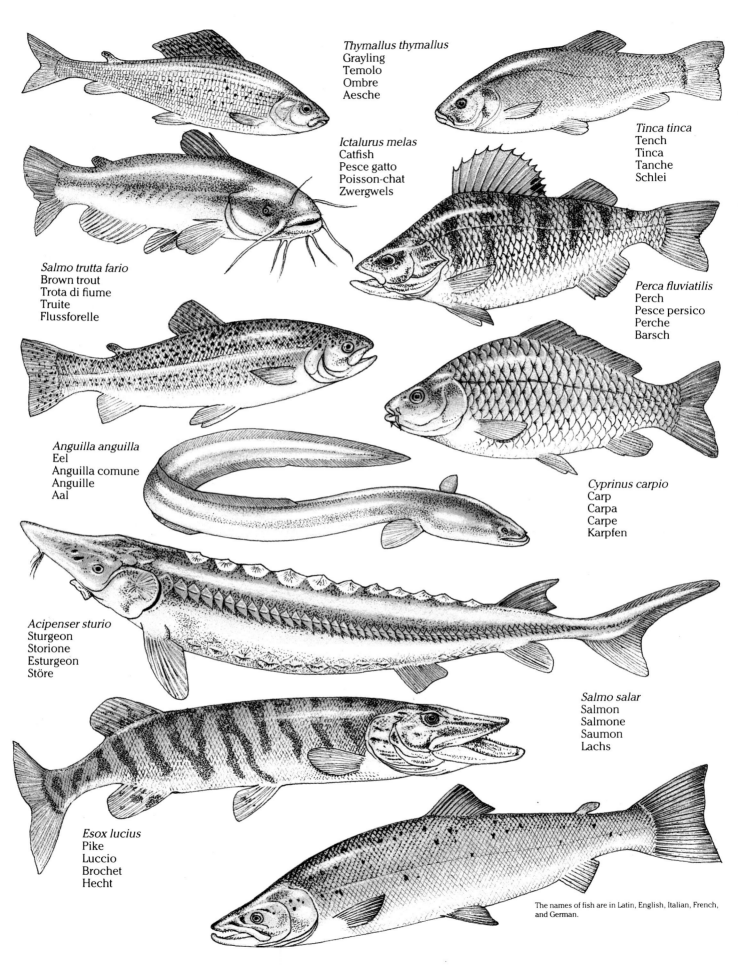

Thymallus thymallus
Grayling
Temolo
Ombre
Aesche

Ictalurus melas
Catfish
Pesce gatto
Poisson-chat
Zwergwels

Salmo trutta fario
Brown trout
Trota di fiume
Truite
Flussforelle

Anguilla anguilla
Eel
Anguilla comune
Anguille
Aal

Acipenser sturio
Sturgeon
Storione
Esturgeon
Störe

Esox lucius
Pike
Luccio
Brochet
Hecht

Tinca tinca
Tench
Tinca
Tanche
Schlei

Perca fluviatilis
Perch
Pesce persico
Perche
Barsch

Cyprinus carpio
Carp
Carpa
Carpe
Karpfen

Salmo salar
Salmon
Salmone
Saumon
Lachs

The names of fish are in Latin, English, Italian, French, and German.

Kedgeree

Preparation: 1½ hours

125 g/4 oz butter
50 g/2 oz plain flour
300 ml/10 fl oz fumet (page 181)
125 ml/4 fl oz single cream

salt and pepper
1 600-g/1¼-lb salmon steak
1 small onion
150 g/5 oz long-grain rice
1 tbsp curry powder
2 hard-boiled eggs

1   Make a white sauce: melt half the butter in a saucepan and stir in the flour. Cook over low heat for 1 minute. Gradually add the fumet, bring to the boil, and add the cream. Cook for 3 minutes, stirring with a whisk. Season with salt and pepper.

2   Skin and fillet the salmon and cut into 5-cm/2-in chunks.

3   Place the salmon pieces in a frying pan with 2 tablespoons water and 25 g/1 oz butter and heat for 10 minutes. Season with salt.

4   Chop the onion and fry in the remaining butter. Add the rice and stir for 2 minutes. Pour in 500 ml/18 fl oz boiling water and 1 teaspoon salt. Bring to the boil, lower the heat, and cook for 15 minutes.

5   Stir the curry powder and pepper into the white sauce. Add the salmon and cook for 2 minutes. Chop the hard-boiled eggs. Spoon the rice on to a heated serving dish, top with the egg, salmon, and curry-flavoured sauce.

Suggested menu

Freshwater crayfish à la nage
Kedgeree
Raspberry Bavarian cream

Suggested wines

Ischia Bianco, Bianchello del Metauro (Italy); Muscadet (France); Californian Pinot Blanc (U.S.A.); Rhine Riesling (Germany).

Gravlax

Preparation: 1 hour
(+ 1 day for the
salmon to stand)

bunch dill
5 peppercorns
900 g/2 lb fresh salmon

40 g/1½ oz sugar
1 tbsp sea salt
2 tbsp Dijon mustard
2 tbsp white wine
  vinegar
125 ml/4 fl oz oil
1 lemon

Suggested menu

Gravlax
New England clam chowder
Wild strawberries and ice cream

Suggested wines

Spumante Champenois del Trentino, Terlano
dell'Alto Adige (Italy); Champagne (France);
Californian Pinot Blanc (U.S.A.); Rhine Sylvaner
(Germany).

1   Rinse and dry the dill and crush the peppercorns.

2   Remove the head from the salmon and cut the fish in half. Remove the backbone using a sharp knife and leave the skin intact. Rinse and dry well.

3   In a small bowl mix together 3 tablespoons sugar, the salt, and the crushed peppercorns.

4   Place half the salmon, skin side down, in a long shallow dish and sprinkle with 1 tablespoon chopped dill and the mixture of salt, sugar, and pepper. Place the other half, skin side up, on top.

5   Wrap in foil, cover with another plate and place a 3-kg/6½-lb weight on top. Refrigerate for at least 24 hours. Turn after 12 hours, spooning the juices over the salmon.

6   Place the salmon on a chopping board and slice off thin pieces diagonally.

7   Prepare the sauce: mix together the mustard, remaining sugar, and vinegar. Blend in the oil gradually. Add the remaining chopped dill.

8   Arrange the slices on a serving dish, cover with the sauce, and garnish with lemon wedges. Serve any remaining sauce separately.

Coulibiac of salmon

Preparation: 1½ hours

250 g/9 oz fresh salmon
125 g/4 oz butter
salt and pepper
½ tsp paprika
½ tsp dried dill
4 tbsp white wine
½ lemon, 3 shallots
50 g/2 oz rice

150 ml/5 fl oz chicken
  stock
3 eggs (2 hard-boiled)
1 tbsp parsley
175 g/6 oz mushrooms
2 tbsp chives
400 g/14 oz puff
  pastry (page 181)
sour cream (optional)

Suggested menu

Seafood salad
Coulibiac of salmon
Floating islands

Suggested wines

Greco di Tufo, Sylvaner dell'Alto Adige (Italy);
Montrachet (France); Californian Chardonnay
(U.S.A.); Rhine Riesling (Germany).

1   Cut the salmon into chunks and place in a buttered roasting tin. Sprinkle with salt, paprika, and dill. Pour the wine and juice of half a lemon over the salmon. Cover with foil and place in a preheated oven (180°C/350°F/mark 4) for 15 minutes.

2   Melt a quarter of the butter in a small saucepan and brown two chopped shallots for 1 minute. Add the rice, stir for 1 minute, then pour in the stock and cook for 15 minutes, adding more boiling water as necessary.

3   Stir into the rice two chopped hard-boiled eggs, the parsley, salt and pepper.

4   Melt 25 g/1 oz butter in another pan; add the remaining finely chopped shallot and the sliced mushrooms and cook for 6 minutes. Sprinkle with salt and the chopped chives.

5   Roll out the pastry into a rectangle 5 mm/¼ in thick. Arrange alternate layers of rice, salmon, and mushrooms in the centre, leaving a generous amount of pastry to fold over.

6   Brush down one side of the pastry with beaten egg. Fold over the other side to enclose the filling and press down gently to seal the edge.

7   Place the salmon roll on a buttered baking tray. Cut decorative leaves with any remaining pastry. Leave two holes for the steam to escape, then brush with beaten egg. Leave to stand for 20 to 30 minutes. Bake at 200°C/400°F/mark 6 for 10 minutes, then lower to 190°C/375°F/mark 5 for 30 minutes.

8   Leave to cool for 15 minutes, then pour melted butter into the holes. Serve with more melted butter or sour cream.

Marinated salmon

Preparation: 30 minutes (+ 2 hours for the salmon to stand and 24 hours for marinating)

1 1-kg/2¼-lb salmon
salt
2 onions

½ red chilli pepper
2 bay leaves
1 tbsp curry powder
½ tsp turmeric
6 peppercorns
500 ml/18 fl oz white wine vinegar
1 tbsp sugar

1   Clean the salmon and cut into slices.

2   Sprinkle with salt and leave to stand for 2 hours.

3   Finely slice the onions and chilli pepper.

4   Steam the slices of salmon for 4 minutes and season with salt.

5   Place the sliced onion, bay leaves, chilli pepper, curry powder, turmeric, peppercorns, vinegar, and sugar in a saucepan. Bring to the boil and simmer for 15 minutes.

6   Place the slices of salmon in a terracotta dish and cover with the hot marinade.

7   Leave to cool, then cover and marinate for 24 hours before serving.

Suggested menu

Marinated salmon
Tench with peas
Peach and Moscato cream with zabaglione

Suggested wines

Pino Bianco di Franciacorta, Torbato (Italy); Muscadet (France); Californian Pinot Blanc (U.S.A.); Moselle Riesling (Germany).

124

Salmon mousse

Preparation: 1 hour
(+ 5 hours for the
mousse to set)

400 g/14 oz fresh
  salmon, in one piece
500 ml/18 fl oz *court-
  bouillon* (page 181)
2 level tbsp gelatine

3 tbsp dry sherry
2 tbsp lemon juice
salt and pepper
200 ml/7 fl oz double
  cream
3 egg whites
2 tbsp oil
gherkins
1 lemon

1   Place the salmon in a casserole; pour in the *court-bouillon*, cover with foil and bake in a preheated oven at 180°C/350°F/ mark 4 for 20 minutes.

2   Leave the salmon to cool slightly. Remove and discard the skin and bones. Cut into pieces and place in a blender or food processor. Dissolve the gelatine over gentle heat in 125 ml/4 fl oz *court-bouillon* and pour into the blender.

3   Add the sherry, lemon juice, and salt and pepper and liquidize until smooth.

4   Whip the cream until firm but not too stiff. Beat the egg whites until stiff and fold both into the salmon mixture.

5   Brush the inside of a large mould or individual ramekins with oil, pour in the mousse, and chill in the refrigerator for at least 5 hours.

6   Turn the mousse out on to a serving dish and garnish with sliced gherkins and lemon.

Suggested menu

Salmon mousse
Clam fritters
Hazelnut ice cream log

Suggested wines

Sauvignon del Collio, Spumante Champenois del Trentino (Italy); Champagne (France); Californian Chardonnay (U.S.A.); Pinot Riesling (Australia).

Blinis with caviare

Preparation: 1 hour
(+ 5½ hours for
making the batter)

5 g/¼ oz fresh, or
  ¼ tsp dried yeast
50 g/2 oz plain flour
200 ml/7 fl oz milk

1 egg, separated
50 g/2 oz butter
40 g/1½ oz
  buckwheat flour
½ tsp sugar
125 ml/4 fl oz sour
  cream
80 g/3 oz caviare

1   Dissolve the yeast in 125 ml/4 fl oz warm water; stir and leave to stand for 10 minutes. In a large bowl mix together the flour with the yeast and water and half the warm milk. Stir thoroughly, cover, and leave to stand at room temperature for 3 hours.

2   Stir in the egg yolk, the remaining warm milk, half the butter (melted), the buckwheat flour, salt, and sugar. Mix well, cover, and leave to stand for a further 2 hours.

3   Stir in half the sour cream and the stiffly beaten egg white a spoonful at a time. Leave to stand for 30 minutes.

4   Brush six small baking tins with the remaining melted butter.

5   Pour 3 tablespoons of batter into each tin. Bake for 20 minutes in a preheated oven at 180°C/350°F/mark 4 until the blinis are slightly puffed up.

6   Arrange the blinis on a serving dish; garnish with a little caviare and serve with the remaining sour cream and extra melted butter.

Suggested menu

Blinis with caviare
Spiny lobster Catalan style
Hazelnut ice cream log

Suggested wines

Terlano dell'Alto Adige, Ribolla dei Colli Orientali del Friuli (Italy); Montrachet (France); Californian Johannisberg Riesling (U.S.A.); Rhine Sylvaner (Germany).

Shad with sorrel

Preparation: 1 hour

275 g/10 oz sorrel
50 g/2 oz butter
2 shallots
salt
pepper
3 tbsp cream

2 hard-boiled eggs
1 tbsp chopped
  parsley
1 1-kg/2¼-lb shad
125 ml/4 fl oz white wine

Serve with: beurre blanc
(page 181)

Suggested menu

Sardines in 'saòr'
Shad with sorrel
Almond squares

Suggested wines

Riesling Renano dei Colli Orientali del Friuli,
Montecarlo Bianco (Italy); Graves Blanc
(France); Californian Pinot Blanc (U.S.A.);
Sauvignon Blanc (South Africa).

1 Rinse, dry, and finely chop the sorrel.

2 Melt 40 g/1½ oz butter in a frying pan and fry the finely chopped shallots for 4 minutes.

3 Add the sorrel and cook for about 10 minutes until the water from the sorrel has evaporated.

4 Sprinkle with salt and pepper and add the cream. Bring to the boil and cook for 1 minute.

5 Chop the hard-boiled eggs and add to the mixture in the pan together with the chopped parsley.

6 Clean and rinse the shad. Fill with the mixture and sew up carefully with kitchen thread.

7 Place the fish in a buttered roasting tin, dot with the remaining butter, and pour over the wine. Cover with buttered foil.

8 Bake in a preheated oven at 190°C/375°F/mark 5 for 25 minutes, basting occasionally with the cooking juices. Serve with beurre blanc.

129

Shad with fresh dates

Preparation: 1½ hours

1 1.2-kg/2¾-lb shad
50 g/2 oz blanched
  almonds
225 g/8 oz fresh dates

½ onion
50 g/2 oz semolina
salt
½ tbsp sugar
pinch ginger
50 g/2 oz butter
pinch cinnamon

1   Clean, rinse, and dry the shad.

2   Chop the almonds, pit the dates, and finely slice the onion.

3   Cook the semolina in 200 ml/7 fl oz water for 10 minutes. Allow to cool.

4   In a bowl mix together the almonds, sugar, semolina, ginger, half the butter (melted), and a pinch of pepper. Stuff the fish with this mixture and sew up with kitchen thread.

5   Butter an ovenproof dish. Arrange the onion slices in the bottom and place the fish on top. Dot with butter, add 125 ml/ 4 fl oz water, salt and pepper, and bake in a preheated oven at 180°C/ 350°F/mark 4 for 20 minutes. Arrange the dates around the fish.

6   Turn the oven up to 200°C/400°F/mark 6 until the cooking juices have evaporated and the skin is crisp. Sprinkle with cinnamon.

Suggested menu

Spaghetti with clams
Shad with fresh dates
Pineapple ice cream

Suggested wines

Pinot dell'Oltrepò Pavese, Torbato (Italy);
Graves Blanc (France); Californian Pinot Blanc (U.S.A.); Riesling (Australia).

Braised sturgeon

Preparation: 1 hour

4 225-g/8-oz sturgeon
  steaks
8 tbsp oil
salt and black pepper
200 ml/7 fl oz white wine
1 stick celery

1 onion
200 g/7 oz tinned
  tomatoes
1 bay leaf
1 clove garlic
2 anchovies
black pepper
chopped parsley

1   Rinse and dry the fish steaks. Heat the oil in a frying pan and cook the steaks for 5 minutes on each side. Sprinkle with salt, pour in half the wine, and simmer for 5 minutes. Remove the steaks and keep warm.

2   Finely chop the celery and cut the onion into thin rings. Cook for 5 minutes in the oil used for frying the fish.

3   Add the chopped tomatoes, the remaining wine, bay leaf, and crushed garlic and cook for 15 minutes.

4   Return the steaks to the pan and add the finely chopped anchovies and black pepper. Cook for a further 10 to 15 minutes.

5   Serve each steak with the tomato sauce and sprinkle with chopped parsley.

Suggested menu

Scallops in white wine
Braised sturgeon
Strawberries and bananas au citron

Suggested wines

Orvieto, Pinot Bianco di Franciacorta (Italy); Meursault (France); Californian Pinot Blanc (U.S.A.); Chardonnay (Australia).

Stuffed pike

Preparation: 1¼ hours
(+ 45 minutes for
soaking the prunes)

15 dried prunes
1 1-kg/2¼-lb pike

125 g/4 oz long-grain
    rice
salt and pepper
3 hard-boiled eggs
50 g/2 oz butter
dried breadcrumbs

Suggested menu

Prawn cocktail
Stuffed pike
Flambéed pineapple

Suggested wines

Lugana, Montecarlo Bianco (Italy); Chassagne
Montrachet (France); Californian Chardonnay
(U.S.A.); Fumé Blanc (South Africa).

1   Soak the prunes in warm water for 45 minutes. Drain them, remove and discard the stones; chop half of them coarsely.

2   Remove the scales, clean, rinse, and dry the pike. Sprinkle with salt.

3   Cook the rice in boiling salted water for 12 to 15 minutes or until tender. Chop the hard-boiled eggs.

4   Stuff the pike with a mixture of rice, egg, the drained chopped prunes, salt and pepper, and half the butter.

5   Sew up the cavity of the fish with kitchen thread.

6   Coat the fish in breadcrumbs.

7   Place in a buttered roasting tin and dot with the remaining butter.

8   Bake in a preheated oven at 150°C/300°F/mark 2 for 15 minutes, then raise the heat to 200°C/400°F/mark 6 for a further 10 minutes or until cooked. Remove the thread. Serve on a bed of rice and garnish with the remaining prunes.

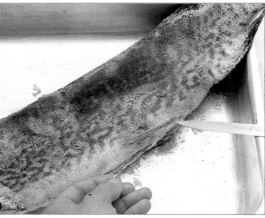

Pike quenelles

Preparation: 30 minutes

1 600-g/1¼-lb pike
40 g/1½ oz butter
50 g/2 oz plain flour
2 eggs
2 egg whites

salt
pepper
150 ml/5 fl oz double
  cream
pinch nutmeg

Serve with: Nantua sauce
(page 182)

Suggested menu

Pike quenelles
Turbot with scampi sauce
Rhubarb soufflé

Suggested wines

Trebbiano di Romagna, Torgiano Bianco (Italy);
Chablis (France); Californian Sauvignon Blanc
(U.S.A.); Moselle Riesling (Germany).

1 Clean and fillet the pike.

2 Heat the butter with 100 ml/3½ fl oz water in a small saucepan. Bring to the boil, remove from the heat, and stir in the flour. Return to the heat for 1 minute, then remove and stir in an egg. Allow to cool.

3 Cut the fillets into pieces and blend in a blender or food processor with a whole egg, two egg whites, the mixture from the small saucepan, and salt and pepper.

4 Add the cream and nutmeg and blend for 30 seconds.

5 Pour the mixture through a fine metal strainer.

6 Shape the mixture into quenelles using two spoons: dip the spoons in water to stop the mixture from sticking and shape into oblongs. Lower the quenelles into gently simmering salted water.

7 Cook for 10 to 15 minutes. Remove with a slotted spoon and drain on kitchen paper.

8 Arrange the quenelles in an ovenproof dish. Cover with a little Nantua sauce and place in a preheated oven at 190°C/375°F/mark 5 for 10 minutes.

Trout au bleu

Preparation: 40 minutes

4 live or freshly killed
    trout, total weight
    1 kg/2¼ lb
1 onion
1 carrot
1 stick celery

500 ml/18 fl oz white wine
125 ml/4 fl oz wine vinegar
1 bouquet garni (bay
    leaf and thyme)
8 black peppercorns
salt

Serve with: Hollandaise
sauce (page 182)

1   Ideally, live fish should be used to produce the characteristic blue colour as the fish are cooked. If live trout are not available, it is essential to clean the fish without rinsing them.

2   Fill a large saucepan one-third full of water and add the chopped vegetables, the wine, vinegar, bouquet garni, peppercorns, and plenty of salt. Simmer for 20 minutes.

3   Lower the trout carefully into the *court-bouillon* and simmer for 4 to 7 minutes.

4   Turn off the heat and leave to stand for a few minutes in the *court-bouillon.*

5   Arrange on a heated serving dish with boiled or steamed potatoes, melted butter, or Hollandaise sauce.

Suggested menu

Scallops in white wine
Trout au bleu
Peach and Moscato cream with zabaglione

Suggested wines

Lugana, Bianchello del Metauro (Italy); Bourgogne Blanc (France); Californian Chenin Blanc (U.S.A.); Chardonnay (Australia).

Anguilles au vert

Preparation: 1 hour

125 g/4 oz fresh sorrel
2 tbsp chopped
  parsley
6 leaves tarragon
3 leaves sage

2 eels, total weight
  1 kg/2¼ lb
50 g/2 oz butter
salt and pepper
300 ml/10 fl oz white wine
2 egg yolks
1½ tbsp lemon juice

1   Rinse and finely chop the sorrel. Chop the parsley, tarragon, and sage.

2   Skin the eels (page 187). Rinse and cut into 5-cm/2-in pieces.

3   Brown the pieces of eel in the butter for 5 minutes. Add the sorrel and other chopped herbs. Season with salt and pepper and pour in the wine.

4   Bring to the boil, lower the heat, and simmer for 15 minutes. Transfer the pieces of eel to a serving dish.

5   Beat the egg yolks with a little of the cooking liquid, then pour into the saucepan.

6   Heat gently for 3 minutes, stirring constantly, until the sauce thickens. Add the lemon juice.

7   Pour the sauce over the eel and leave to cool before serving.

Suggested menu

Crab Venetian style
Anguilles au vert
Pineapple Bavarian cream with puréed
  strawberries

Suggested wines

Ribolla dei Colli Orientali del Friuli, Vernaccia di San Gimignano (Italy); Sancerre (France); Californian Johannisberg Riesling (U.S.A.); Rhine Riesling (Germany).

Eel stew

Preparation: 1¼ hours
(+ 1 hour for soaking
the prunes)

1 ham bone
125 g/4 oz carrots
½ onion
3 sticks celery
175 g/6 oz cauliflower

125 g/4 oz dried prunes
salt and pepper
1 450-g/1-lb eel
125 ml/4 fl oz wine
   vinegar
bouquet garni
150 g/5 oz plain flour
2 eggs
25 g/1 oz butter

Suggested menu

Eel stew
Tuna Charterhouse style
Rhubarb soufflé

Suggested wines

Sylvaner dell'Alto Adige, Montecarlo Bianco
(Italy); Gewürztraminer d'Alsace (France);
Californian Gewürztraminer (U.S.A.); Müller
Thurgau (New Zealand).

1　Cover the ham bone with water in a large saucepan and simmer for 20 minutes, removing the scum every so often.

2　Dice the carrots, onion, and celery and cut the cauliflower into florets.

3　Add the vegetables in the order of cooking time required: carrots, celery, onion, and after 5 minutes the cauliflower and soaked prunes. Add salt and cook for 15 minutes.

4　Skin the eel and cut into pieces. Place in a saucepan with the vinegar, bouquet garni, and a little water and cook for 10 minutes.

5　Remove the ham bone from the stock. Cut off any ham left on the bone and add to the stock.

6　Prepare the 'dumplings' by working together the flour, eggs butter, and salt. Add a little water if necessary.

7　Work the dough for 5 minutes, roll into cylinders and chop into small pieces. Cook in boiling salted water for 5 minutes.

8　Add the eel and 'dumplings' to the vegetable stock. Cook for a further 3 minutes, add pepper, and serve.

Eel pie

Preparation: 1 hour
20 minutes

1 1-kg/2¼-lb eel
80 g/3 oz butter
1 large shallot
200 ml/7 fl oz Marsala
pinch nutmeg

1 tbsp chopped
    parsley
salt and pepper
50 g/2 oz plain flour
juice of ½ lemon
2 hard-boiled eggs
50 g/2 oz frozen
    shortcrust pastry

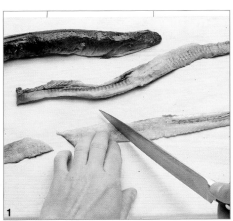

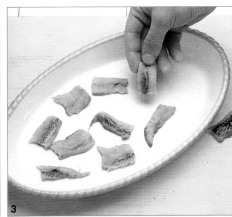

1   Rinse and skin the eel. Divide in half lengthwise, remove the backbone, and cut into 5-cm/2-in pieces.

2   Melt 25 g/1 oz butter in a frying pan and brown the finely chopped shallot. Add the Marsala, nutmeg, parsley, 200 ml/7 fl oz water, salt and pepper, and cook for 4 minutes.

3   Place the pieces of eel in a large buttered ovenproof dish.

4   Melt the remaining butter and stir in the flour. Cook gently for 1 minute.

5   Stir in the mixture from the frying pan and add the lemon juice. Bring to the boil, stirring constantly, and cook for 3 minutes.

6   Pour the sauce over the eel. Place the slices of hard-boiled egg on top and cover with the pastry. Bake in a preheated oven at 230°C/450°F/mark 8 for 10 minutes, then lower to 180°C/350°F/mark 4 for 30 minutes.

Suggested menu

Soused herrings
Eel pie
Pear flan

Suggested wines

Lugana, Soave (Italy); Pouilly-Fuissé (France); Californian Chardonnay (U.S.A.); Moselle Riesling (Germany).

Eel Venetian style

Preparation: 1 hour

1 1-kg/2¼-lb eel
4 tbsp oil
salt
125 ml/4 fl oz white
  wine
2 tbsp vinegar

1 bay leaf
1 onion
300 g/10 oz tinned
  tomatoes
1 clove garlic
black pepper
1 tbsp chopped
  parsley

Suggested menu

Prawn cocktail
Eel Venetian style
Strawberries and bananas au citron

Suggested wines

Spumante Champenois dell'Oltrepò Pavese,
Sylvaner dell'Alto Adige (Italy); Sancerre
(France); Californian Sauvignon Blanc (U.S.A.);
Rhine Riesling (South Africa).

1   Clean and skin the eel and cut into 5-cm/2-in pieces.

2   Heat 1 tablespoon oil in a frying pan; add the eel, sprinkle with salt, pour in half the wine, the vinegar, and the crumbled bay leaf. Cook for 4 minutes.

3   Remove from the heat and drain the eel on kitchen paper.

4   Finely chop the onion and brown for 2 minutes in 2 tablespoons oil.

5   Add the chopped tomatoes and cook for 10 minutes.

6   Pour the sauce through a fine strainer into a bowl.

7   Return the eel to the pan; pour in the remaining wine and cook for 2 minutes before adding the tomato sauce. Cook for a further 5 minutes.

8   Finely chop the garlic. Heat in 1 tablespoon oil for 2 minutes, then pour over the eel. Sprinkle with salt and pepper and chopped parsley before serving.

Carp Jewish style

Preparation: 1¼ hours
(+ 2 hours for chilling)

1 1.2-kg/2¾-lb carp
80 g/3 oz blanched
    almonds
1 onion, 2 shallots
12 tbsp oil, 2 tbsp plain flour

1 tbsp sugar
300 ml/10 fl oz fumet
    (page 181)
80 g/3 oz sultanas
bouquet garni
1 clove garlic
salt and pepper
1 tbsp chopped parsley

Suggested menu

Deep-fried soft-shell crabs
Carp Jewish style
Pear flan

Suggested wines

Pinot Champenois di Franciacorta, Pinot Grigio
dell'Alto Adige (Italy); Montrachet (France);
Californian Blanc de Noirs (U.S.A.); Sauvignon
Blanc (New Zealand).

1 Clean and rinse the carp.

2 Chop the almonds into thin slivers.

3 Finely chop the onion and shallots.

4 Pour half the oil into a frying pan. Add the chopped onion and shallots and fry for 2 minutes.

5 Stir in the flour and sugar and cook for 2 minutes before adding the fumet, almonds, and sultanas.

6 Place the carp in a fish kettle with the bouquet garni and crushed garlic. Pour over the sauce.

7 Heat gently for a few minutes before seasoning with salt and pepper. Cook over moderate heat for a further 30 minutes.

8 Drain the carp and place on a serving dish. Reduce the cooking liquid by boiling vigorously. Discard the bouquet garni and add the remaining oil, stirring with a balloon whisk. Adjust the seasoning and allow to cool before pouring the sauce over the fish. Chill for at least 2 hours and sprinkle with chopped parsley before serving.

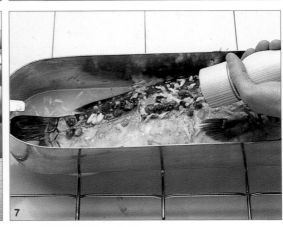

Carp Polish style

Preparation: 1 hour
(+ 1 hour for the carp
to stand)

1 1-kg/2¼-lb carp
salt
1 stick celery
1 small onion
2 sprigs parsley

4 cloves
40 g/1½ oz butter
30 g/1 oz plain flour
125 ml/4 fl oz red wine
1 tbsp wine vinegar
4 pieces spiced bread
1 lemon
2 tbsp sultanas
2 tbsp slivered almonds

Suggested menu

Prawn pilaf
Carp Polish style
Passion fruit sorbet

Suggested wines

Greco di Tufo, Ribolla dei Colli Orientali del
Friuli (Italy); Californian Sauvignon Blanc
(U.S.A.); Montrachet (France); Rhine Sylvaner
(Germany).

1 Clean and rinse the carp and cut into 4 steaks. Sprinkle with salt and leave to stand for 1 hour.

2 Chop the celery and slice the onion. Place in a saucepan with 1.5 litres/ 2½ pints water, the parsley, and cloves and cook for 15 minutes.

3 Add the fish steaks, bring to the boil, lower the heat, and simmer for 10 minutes.

4 Remove the steaks with a slotted spoon and keep warm.

5 Strain the stock through a fine sieve and reduce by boiling vigorously for 10 minutes.

6 Melt the butter in a saucepan, stir in the flour, and cook for 2 to 3 minutes.

7 Add the wine, vinegar, stock, and pieces of spiced bread and cook for 4 minutes.

8 Strain the sauce and reheat. Add the lemon juice, sultanas, and almonds; stir well and pour over the fish steaks.

Deep-fried catfish

Preparation: 45
minutes

4 catfish, total weight
 1 kg/2¼ lb
salt
pepper

1 egg
125 ml/4 fl oz milk
125 g/4 oz masa
 harina (maize flour)
125 g/4 oz lard
gherkins
coleslaw

Suggested menu

Prawn risotto
Deep-fried catfish
Pear flan

Suggested wines

Montecarlo Bianco, Lugana (Italy); Pinot
d'Alsace (France); Californian Pinot Blanc
(U.S.A.); Rhine Riesling (Germany).

1 Clean the fish and cut into fillets but do not skin.

2 Cut each fillet diagonally into three.

3 Sprinkle with salt and pepper.

4 Beat the egg and milk together and dip each fillet in the batter.

5 Dip each piece in the flour, pressing to make sure they are evenly coated.

6 Melt the lard in a frying pan and when it is hot fry the pieces of fish for 4 minutes on each side.

7 Drain well on kitchen paper to absorb excess fat.

8 Serve with gherkins and coleslaw.

Perch with sage

Preparation: 40 minutes

4 perch, total weight 1.2 kg/2¾ lb
plain flour

1 egg
salt
50 ml/2 fl oz milk
dried breadcrumbs
80 g/3 oz butter
12 leaves sage

Suggested menu

Freshwater crayfish à la nage
Perch with sage
Peach and Moscato cream with zabaglione

Suggested wines

Gavi, Riesling dell'Oltrepò Pavese (Italy);
Pouilly-Fuissé (France); Californian Blanc de
Blancs (U.S.A.); Fumé Blanc (South Africa).

1   Fillet the fish carefully using a very sharp filleting knife.

2   Coat the fillets lightly with flour.

3   Beat the egg, add a pinch of salt, and beat with the milk.

4   Dip the fillets first in the beaten egg mixture, then in breadcrumbs, pressing well to make them stick.

5   Melt 50 g/2 oz butter in a frying pan with 4 sage leaves.

6   Place the fillets in a single layer in the frying pan and cook for 4 minutes on each side. Add the remaining sage leaves and cook for a further 2 minutes. Season with salt.

7   Remove the fillets, melt the remaining butter in the same frying pan and heat until golden brown and foaming.

8   Pour the butter over the fillets and serve immediately.

Tench with peas

Preparation: 1 hour

4 tbsp vinegar
2 tench, total weight
  1.2 kg/2¾ lb
50 g/2 oz butter
4 tbsp oil
2 tbsp plain flour

salt and pepper
200 ml/7 fl oz white wine
225 g/8 oz button
  mushrooms
225 g/8 oz shelled
  peas
2 ripe tomatoes
4 leaves sage

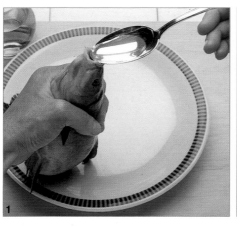
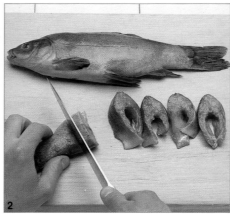

1   Pour 2 tablespoons vinegar into each fish to remove the slightly muddy smell.

2   After 10 minutes, clean and rinse the fish and cut into slices. Melt half the butter and half the oil in a frying pan. Dip the slices of fish in flour and place in the pan. Sprinkle with salt, pour in half the wine, then fry for 5 minutes on each side.

3   Remove the pieces of fish and keep warm. Add the remaining oil and butter to the frying pan together with the sliced mushrooms, peas, and peeled and chopped tomatoes.

4   Season with salt, add the sage leaves and remaining wine, and cook for 10 minutes.

5   Return the fish to the pan and add half a ladle of hot water.

6   Adjust the seasoning and cook until the fish is tender and the sauce slightly reduced. Sprinkle. with salt and pepper.

Suggested menu

Potted crab
Tench with peas
Rhubarb soufflé

Suggested wines

Sauvignon del Collio, Sylvaner dell'Alto Adige (Italy); Graves Blanc (France); Californian Fumé Blanc (U.S.A.); Chardonnay (South Africa).

Lithuanian fish balls

Preparation: 1 hour
(+ 3 hours for the
fumet to set)

1 kg/2¼ lb assorted
   fish (carp, pike, etc.)
1 slice bread
50 ml/2 fl oz milk

1 onion
2 eggs, beaten
salt and pepper
1 litre/1¾ pints fumet
   (page 181)
1 carrot
1 tbsp grated
   horseradish

1   Clean and fillet the fish and chop coarsely.

2   Soak the slice of bread in the milk.

3   Finely chop the onion; mix with the fish, the beaten eggs, the drained and squeezed bread, and salt and pepper.

4   Mix well and shape into small balls.

5   Cook the fish balls in the gently simmering fumet for 30 minutes.

6   Slice the carrot, add to the fumet, and cook for 4 minutes.

7   Remove the fish balls and carrots with a slotted spoon and reduce the fumet by boiling vigorously for 10 minutes. Strain and refrigerate for 3 hours until set.

8   Serve the fish balls with the chopped gelled fumet. Garnish with slices of carrot and grated horseradish.

Suggested menu

Deep-fried soft-shell crabs
Lithuanian fish balls
Peach and Moscato cream with zabaglione

Suggested wines

Terlano dell'Alto Adige, Riesling Renano dei Colli Orientali del Friuli (Italy); Bordeaux Blanc (France); Californian Chardonnay (U.S.A.); Sauvignon Blanc (New Zealand).

Molluscs

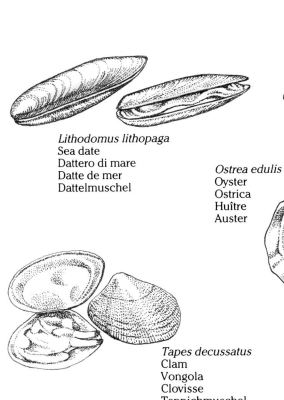

Lithodomus lithopaga
Sea date
Dattero di mare
Datte de mer
Dattelmuschel

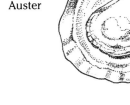

Ostrea edulis
Oyster
Ostrica
Huître
Auster

Sepia officinalis
Cuttlefish
Seppia
Seiche
Tintenfisch

Tapes decussatus
Clam
Vongola
Clovisse
Teppichmuschel

Pecten jacobaeus
Scallop
Conchiglia di San Giacomo
Coquille Saint-Jacques
Jacobmuschel

Octopus vulgaris
Octopus
Polpo comune
Poulpe
Gemeiner Krake

Mytilus edulis
Mussel
Mitilo
Moule
Miesmuschel

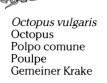

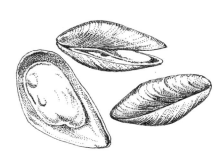

Loligo vulgaris
Squid
Calamaro
Calmar
Gewöhnlicher Kalmar

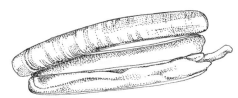

Solen vagina
Razor clam
Cannolicchio
Couteau
Messerscheide

The names of fish are in Latin, English, Italian, French, and German.

Coquilles Saint-Jacques à la provençale

Preparation: 20 minutes
(+ 1 hour for cleaning
the scallops)

1 kg/2¼ lb scallops
salt and pepper
80 g/3 oz butter

3 tbsp plain flour
2 shallots
1 tbsp oil
1 clove garlic
125 ml/4 fl oz white wine
1 tbsp chopped
  parsley

1   Leave the scallops under cold running water for 1 hour; prise them open and remove the white meat and coral. Reserve the shells. Discard the black gristly parts. Cut the white cushion in two and sprinkle with salt and pepper.

2   Heat 50 g/2 oz butter in a frying pan. Lightly coat the scallops in flour and fry gently, a few at a time, for 3 minutes until golden brown. Cook the corals for 1½ to 2 minutes only.

3   Finely chop the shallots and fry for 2 minutes in the remaining butter and oil. Add the garlic, cook for one minute, then add to the scallops. Pour in the wine.

4   Cook over moderate heat for another 3 minutes.

5   Remove the scallops and keep warm. Reduce the sauce by boiling vigorously.

6   Pour the sauce over the scallops, sprinkle with chopped parsley, and serve in warmed shells.

Suggested menu

Coquilles Saint-Jacques à la provençale
John Dory with vegetables
Almond squares

Suggested wines

Ischia Bianco, Lugana (Italy); Pouilly-Fuissé (France); Californian Johannisberg Riesling (U.S.A.); Moselle Riesling (Germany).

Scallops in white wine

Preparation: 40 minutes
(+ 1 hour for cleaning
the scallops)

16 scallops
2 leeks

50 g/2 oz butter
salt
200 ml/7 fl oz Riesling
(or other medium-
dry white wine)
pepper

1 Leave the scallops under cold running water for 1 hour. Prise the shells open and cut out the scallop, discarding the black gristly part around the cushion.

2 Cut the white part of the leeks into strips.

3 Melt the butter and fry the leeks briefly. Sprinkle with salt and pour in the wine.

4 Cook gently for 5 minutes. Add the scallops and cook, covered, for a further 5 minutes.

5 Remove the scallops and leeks and keep warm.

6 Reduce the sauce over medium heat. Place a layer of leeks on each plate; top with scallops, sprinkle with pepper, and cover with sauce.

Suggested menu

Scallops in white wine
Sea bass en croûte
Calvados sorbet

Suggested wines

Pinot Bianco di Franciacorta, Riesling dell'Oltrepò Pavese (Italy); Graves Blanc (France); Californian Chardonnay (U.S.A.); Chenin Blanc (South Africa).

Chilled oyster soup

Preparation: 30 minutes (+ 2 hours for chilling)

800 g/1¾ lb oysters
50 g/2 oz butter
2 slices bacon
1 onion
50 g/2 oz plain flour

1 litre/1¾ pints milk
3 tbsp dry sherry
250 ml/9 fl oz single cream
2 tbsp chopped parsley
salt
pepper
½ tsp paprika

1   Prise open the shells over a bowl using a strong, short-bladed knife. Remove the oysters and reserve the liquid.

2   Melt the butter and gently fry the finely chopped bacon and onion for 5 minutes.

3   Sprinkle in the flour and cook for 1 minute, stirring constantly.

4   Add the very hot milk and the reserved oyster liquid. Boil for 3 minutes until thickened.

5   Remove from the heat and add the sherry and cream, stirring thoroughly until well blended.

6   Add the oysters and 1 tablespoon parsley and cook for 5 minutes over moderate heat. Season with salt and pepper.

7   Leave to cool, then refrigerate for 2 hours. Serve in individual bowls, and sprinkle with paprika and chopped parsley.

Suggested menu

Chilled oyster soup
Sole à la meunière
Sablés

Suggested wines

Orvieto, Vermentino (Italy); Muscadet (France); Californian Sauvignon Blanc (U.S.A.); Rhine Riesling (South Africa).

Creamed oysters

Preparation: 30 minutes

32 oysters
300 ml/10 fl oz milk

300 ml/10 fl oz single cream
pinch celery seeds
25 g/1 oz butter
salt and pepper
pinch paprika

1   Prise open the oysters with a short-bladed knife and cut them from the shell. Strain the liquor into a small bowl and reserve.

2   Heat the milk and cream in a small saucepan; add the celery seeds and 2 tablespoons of the oyster liquor and boil for 5 minutes. Strain through a fine sieve.

3   Melt the butter in a separate saucepan. Add the oysters with 2 tablespoons of the reserved liquor and cook gently for 3 minutes. Remove from the heat.

4   Add the milk and cream, season with salt and pepper, and cook for a further 2 minutes.

5   Arrange the oysters in heated bowls and cover with the creamy sauce.

6   Sprinkle with paprika and serve at once.

Suggested menu

Creamed oysters
Stuffed squid
Sablés

Suggested wines

Pinot Bianco di Franciacorta, Riesling Renano dei Colli Orientali del Friuli (Italy); Bourgogne Blanc (France); Californian Sauvignon Blanc (U.S.A.); Chardonnay (New Zealand).

Sea date soup

Preparation: 1 hour
(+ 2 hours for
cleaning the sea dates)

1 kg/2¼ lb sea dates
8 tbsp oil
2 cloves garlic
1½ tbsp chopped
  parsley

pinch Cayenne pepper
200 ml/7 fl oz single
  cream
1 tsp meat extract
200 g/7 oz tinned
  tomatoes
200 ml/7 fl oz white
  wine
salt

Suggested menu

Sea date soup
Lobster Newburg
Apricot soufflé

Suggested wines

Pinot Bianco del Collio, Regaleali Bianco (Italy);
Chablis (France); Californian Chardonnay
(U.S.A.); Chenin Blanc (South Africa).

1   Rinse the sea dates, preferably under running water, for 2 hours, to remove all traces of sand.

2   Drain them and heat for 4 minutes in a covered frying pan until they open. Remove from their shells.

3   Reserve the cooking liquor and strain through a fine sieve.

4   Pour the oil into a frying pan and gently heat the finely chopped garlic.

5   Add 1 tablespoon parsley, the Cayenne pepper, cream, meat extract, tomatoes, wine, and reserved liquor.

6   Cook for 15 minutes, then strain through a fine sieve into a saucepan.

7   Add the sea dates and heat for 2 minutes. Adjust the seasoning. Sprinkle with the remaining chopped parsley and serve with slices of hot fried or toasted bread.

Clam soup

Preparation: 30 minutes (+ 2 hours for cleaning the clams)

1 kg/2¼ lb clams
8 tbsp oil

2 cloves garlic
2 large ripe tomatoes
salt and pepper
1 vegetable stock
    cube
1 tbsp chopped
    parsley

1　Rinse the clams, preferably under running water, for 2 hours to remove all traces of sand.

2　Pour 2 tablespoons oil into a frying pan, add 1 crushed clove of garlic and fry briefly. Remove the garlic, add the drained clams, and cook, covered, for 4 minutes.

3　Shell the clams and keep warm in the strained and reserved cooking liquor.

4　Pour 4 tablespoons oil into a saucepan and add the skinned, seeded, and chopped tomatoes. Sprinkle with salt and cook for 10 minutes. Add the clams with their cooking liquor and 3 ladles vegetable stock.

5　Heat 2 tablespoons oil in a small saucepan; add the finely chopped garlic and parsley, sprinkle with salt and pepper, and add to the clams.

6　Mix well and serve with slices of hot fried or toasted bread.

Suggested menu

Clam soup
Lobster Newburg
Pineapple Bavarian cream with puréed
   strawberries

Suggested wines

Tocai del Collio, Verdicchio dei Castelli di Jesi (Italy); Bourgogne Blanc (France); Californian Johannisberg Riesling (U.S.A.); Chenin Blanc (Australia).

Spaghetti with clams

Preparation: 40 minutes (+ 2 hours for cleaning the clams)

800 g/1¾ lb clams

1 clove garlic
250 g/9 oz spaghetti
salt and pepper
6 tbsp oil
1 tbsp chopped parsley

1   Rinse the clams, preferably under running water, for 2 hours to remove all traces of sand.

2   Drain and heat the clams in a covered saucepan for 4 minutes.

3   Shell the clams, strain and reserve the cooking liquor.

4   Chop the garlic finely.

5   Cook the spaghetti in a large saucepan of boiling salted water for 8 to 10 minutes or until *al dente*. Drain.

6   Heat the oil in a saucepan and fry the garlic for 1 minute.

7   Pour the reserved cooking liquor into a large frying pan and reduce by boiling vigorously for 3 to 4 minutes. Add the clams and heat for 1 minute.

8   Add the spaghetti to the clams, pour in the garlic oil and add the chopped parsley; mix well over medium heat for 1 minute. Sprinkle with black pepper. Serve at once.

Suggested menu

Spaghetti with clams
Turbot with scampi sauce
Flambéed pineapple

Suggested wines

Pinot di Franciacorta, Verdicchio dei Castelli di Jesi (Italy); Montrachet (France); Californian Chenin Blanc (U.S.A.); Chardonnay (South Africa).

Manhattan clam chowder

Preparation: 1 hour 20 minutes (+ 2 hours for cleaning the clams)

1 kg/2¼ lb clams
150 g/5 oz streaky bacon
1 medium onion
1 carrot
1 stick celery
200 g/7 oz tinned tomatoes
1 bay leaf
pinch thyme
salt and pepper
2 small potatoes

1   Rinse the clams, preferably under running water, for 2 hours, to remove all traces of sand.

2   Place the clams in a saucepan; cover and cook for 3 minutes or until the shells open. Strain and reserve the cooking liquid.

3   Remove the clams from their shells.

4   Chop the bacon and fry for 1 minute. Add the chopped onion, carrot, and celery and cook for 5 minutes.

5   Add the tomatoes, bay leaf, thyme, and reserved cooking liquid from the clams. Season with salt and pepper and cook for 6 minutes.

6   Add 4 ladles of water and bring to the boil. Lower the heat, add the peeled and diced potatoes, and simmer for 20 minutes.

7   Add the clams and heat gently for 2 minutes before serving.

Suggested menu

Manhattan clam chowder
Spiny lobster Algerian style
Chilled orange soufflé

Suggested wines

Corvo di Salaparuta, Vermentino (Italy); Pouilly-Fuissé (France); Californian Sauvignon Blanc (U.S.A.); Moselle Riesling (Germany).

Clam fritters

Preparation: 1 hour
(+ 2 hours for
cleaning the clams)

1 kg/2¼ lb clams
2 eggs

25 g/1 oz fresh
  breadcrumbs
salt
pinch Cayenne
  pepper
oil for deep frying

1   Rinse the clams, preferably under running water, for 2 hours to remove all traces of sand.

2   Drain and heat in a covered saucepan for 4 minutes until the shells open. Strain and reserve the cooking liquor.

3   Shell the clams and chop coarsely.

4   Separate the eggs. Beat the yolks and stir in the chopped clams, breadcrumbs and reserved liquor. Add salt and Cayenne pepper.

5   Whisk the egg whites until stiff and fold into the clam mixture.

6   Heat plenty of vegetable oil in a frying pan and, when hot, deep fry spoonfuls of the mixture a few at a time.

7   Remove the fritters when they are crisp and brown.

8   Drain on kitchen paper to remove excess oil.

Suggested menu

Clam fritters
Scampi in tomato and white wine sauce
Sablés

Suggested wines

Sauvignon del Collio, Soave (Italy); Montrachet (France); Californian Johannisberg Riesling (U.S.A.); Moselle Riesling (Germany); Chenin Blanc (Australia).

New England clam chowder

Preparation: 1 hour
(+ 2 hours for
cleaning the clams)

800 g/1¾ lb clams
80 g/3 oz streaky bacon
1 small onion
2 medium potatoes
125ml/4 fl oz milk
125 ml/4 fl oz single
 cream
25 g/1 oz butter
salt
pepper

1   Rinse the clams, preferably under running water, for 2 hours, to remove all traces of sand.

2   Heat the clams in a saucepan for a few minutes until the shells open. Strain and reserve the cooking liquid.

3   Remove the clams from their shells.

4   Chop the bacon and slice the onion.

5   Fry the bacon in a large heavy-bottomed saucepan over high heat for 3 minutes. Add the onion, lower the heat slightly, and cook for 5 minutes.

6   Add the reserved cooking liquid, 500 ml/ 18 fl oz water, and the peeled and diced potatoes. Bring to the boil, lower the heat, and cook for 15 minutes.

7   Stir in the clams, milk, cream, butter, and salt and pepper. Heat gently until just below boiling point. Serve with crackers.

Suggested menu

New England clam chowder
Cuttlefish with peas
Flambéed apricots

Suggested wines

Frascati, Trebbiano di Romagna (Italy); Meursault (France); Californian Chardonnay (U.S.A.); Rhine Riesling (Germany).

Moules marinière

Preparation: 20 minutes (+ 2 hours for cleaning the mussels)

2 kg/4½ lb mussels
1 onion
3 shallots

1 clove garlic
25 g/1 oz butter
250 ml/9 fl oz white wine
½ bay leaf
pinch thyme
black pepper
3 tbsp chopped
    parsley

1   Scrub the mussels thoroughly, removing the beard-like threads, and leave under running water for 2 hours to rinse free of sand.

2   Chop the onion, shallots, and garlic.

3   Melt the butter in a large saucepan and gently fry the onion and shallots until tender. Add the garlic and cook for a further 1 minute.

4   Add the wine, bay leaf, thyme, and black pepper and cook for 2 minutes.

5   Add the mussels and cook for 5 minutes, shaking the pan occasionally, until all the shells have opened. Discard any which have not.

6   Sprinkle with parsley and serve the mussels in bowls with the cooking liquid.

Suggested menu

Moules marinière
Stuffed hake
Pineapple ice cream

Suggested wines

Bianchello del Metauro, Corvo di Salaparuta (Italy); Pinot d'Alsace (France); Californian Pinot Blanc (U.S.A.); Moselle Riesling (Germany).

Cuttlefish with peas

Preparation: 40 minutes

800 g/1¾ lb cuttlefish (or squid)
½ onion
125 ml/4 fl oz white wine

salt and pepper
200 g/7 oz tomatoes
400 g/14 oz shelled peas
½ tsp sugar
sprig rosemary

Suggested menu

Salmon mousse
Cuttlefish with peas
Strawberries with Champagne

Suggested wines

Gavi, Pinot Grigio dell'Alto Adige (Italy); Chablis (France); Californian Chardonnay (U.S.A.); Chenin Blanc (Australia).

1   Remove the central bone of the cuttlefish by pressing in the end of the sac-like body and pulling from the opposite end. The head will pull away, together with the bone, the ink sac, and entrails. Reserve the tentacles and body and discard the rest. Rinse and dry the cuttlefish, rubbing off the purplish skin; cut in half lengthwise and chop into strips 5 cm/2 in long.

2   Finely chop the onion and brown in the oil.

3   After 4 minutes add the strips of cuttlefish and chopped tentacles.

4   Cook for 5 minutes, then pour in the wine. Season with salt, cover, and cook for a further 5 minutes.

5   Add the skinned, seeded, and chopped tomatoes and cook, uncovered, over high heat for 5 minutes.

6   Add the peas and sugar.

7   Cook for a further 15 minutes. Add the rosemary, adjust the seasoning and sprinkle with pepper. Reduce the sauce by boiling vigorously for 1 minute, then serve.

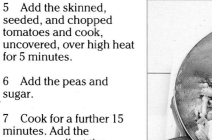

Stewed baby octopus

Preparation: 1 hour

800 g/1¾ lb baby
  octopus
6 tbsp oil
salt and black pepper

4 large ripe tomatoes
150 ml/5 fl oz white
  wine
1 clove garlic
1 tbsp chopped
  parsley

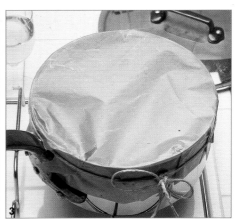

1   Beat the octopus with a rolling pin. Pull away the tentacles and discard the eyes and mouth sections. Rinse and dry the tentacles and body sacs.

2   Heat the oil in a large saucepan; add the octopus, sprinkle with salt, and cook with the seeded and chopped tomatoes for 5 minutes, before adding the wine.

3   Cover the pan with waxed paper, tie with string, then cover with a tightly fitting lid to seal in the flavour.

4   Chop the garlic very finely.

5   Simmer the octopus for 20 minutes. Uncover and add the garlic and parsley.

6   Sprinkle with pepper and cook for a few more minutes before serving.

Suggested menu

Coquilles Saint-Jacques à la provençale
Stewed baby octopus
Chilled orange soufflé

Suggested wines

Regaleali Bianco, Orvieto (Italy); Bordeaux Blanc (France); Californian Chenin Blanc (U.S.A.); Riesling (Australia).

Stuffed squid

Preparation: 1 hour

8 squid, total weight
  800 g/1¾ lb
8 black olives, pitted
1 tbsp capers
2 tbsp chopped
  parsley
2 drops Tabasco

2 drops Worcester-
  shire sauce
1 tbsp breadcrumbs
125 ml/4 fl oz oil
1 clove garlic
2 large tomatoes
salt
pinch oregano
black pepper

Suggested menu

Potted crab
Stuffed squid
Lemon tart

Suggested wines

Sylvaner dell'Alto Adige, Riesling dell'Oltrepò
Pavese (Italy); Gewürztraminer d'Alsace
(France); Californian Gewürztraminer (U.S.A.);
Rhine Riesling (South Africa).

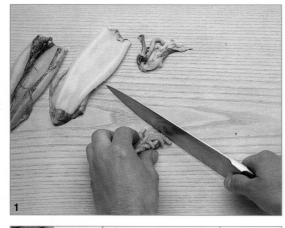

1   Cut off the tentacles, remove and discard the ink sac attached to the head. Pull out and discard the central transparent 'pen' and rub off the purplish outer skin.

2   Chop the tentacles.

3   Finely chop the olives, capers, and parsley.

4   Place all the chopped ingredients, including the tentacles, in a bowl and add 2 drops each of Tabasco and Worcestershire sauce, the breadcrumbs, and 2 tablespoons oil. Mix well.

5   Stuff each squid with a little filling and carefully sew the ends with kitchen thread.

6   Finely chop the garlic and the skinned and seeded tomatoes.

7   Pour the remaining oil into a large frying pan. Gently fry the chopped garlic over very low heat for 2 minutes. Add the chopped tomatoes and cook for a further 2 minutes.

8   Add the stuffed squid and a little salt. Cover and simmer for 20 minutes. Sprinkle with oregano and black pepper and cook for 3 minutes. Serve immediately.

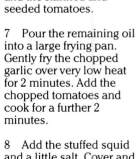

Dessert recipes

Almond squares

125 g/4 oz slivered
almonds
25 g/1 oz plain flour
125 g/4 oz icing sugar
1 egg
2 egg whites
15 g/½ oz butter

Mix the almonds, flour, and sugar in a bowl with the whole egg and egg whites and leave to stand for 30 minutes. Place spoonfuls of the mixture, well spaced out, on a buttered baking tray. Flatten slightly and shape into squares. Bake in a preheated oven at 180°C/350°F/mark 4 for about 8 minutes. When the squares are golden brown remove and place on a wire rack to cool.

Aniseed and almond biscuits

250 g/9 oz blanched
almonds
500 g/1 lb 2 oz plain flour
4 eggs
250 g/9 oz sugar
125 g/4 oz butter
1 tsp dried yeast
1 tsp aniseed
grated rind of 1 lemon
pinch salt
3 tbsp Alkermes (liqueur)
50 g/2 oz icing sugar

Chop the almonds coarsely. Sift the flour into a large bowl. Make a well in the centre and work in the eggs, sugar, softened butter, the yeast, aniseed, lemon rind, and salt. Work the ingredients together until you have a smooth dough. Work in the chopped almonds. Roll out on a floured work surface to 1 cm/½ in thick and cut into biscuit shapes. Bake for 10 minutes at 180°C/350°F/mark 4. Place on a cooling rack, brush with the liqueur and sprinkle with icing sugar.

Apricot soufflé

225 g/8 oz apricots
knob of butter
150 g/5 oz sugar
4 egg whites
125 g/4 oz raspberries
few drops lemon juice

Plunge the apricots for 15 seconds into boiling water and then into cold water. Rub away the skins. Remove the pits; reserve 2 apricots for decoration and liquidize the rest. Butter 4 individual soufflé dishes and sprinkle with sugar. Place 125 g/4 oz sugar and 2 tablespoons water in a saucepan; bring to the boil, add the liquidized apricots, and cook for 3 minutes. Whisk the egg whites until stiff, fold gently into the cooled apricot mixture, and beat for 1 minute. Pour into the soufflé dishes and place in a preheated oven at 170°C/325°F/mark 3 for 20 minutes. Push the raspberries through a nylon sieve and stir in a few drops of lemon juice and the remaining sugar. Mix well and leave to stand. Pour the raspberry sauce into dishes, unmould the soufflés into the centre, and decorate with the reserved sliced apricots.

Calvados sorbet

350 g/12 oz sugar
350 ml/12 fl oz water
400 ml/14 fl oz mineral
water
125 ml/4 fl oz Calvados

Place the sugar and ordinary water in a saucepan over high heat. Stir until the sugar has dissolved. Bring to the boil and leave to cool. Add the Calvados and mineral water, pour into a container, and mix well. Chill in the freezer for at least 1 hour.

Chestnut truffles

700 g/1½ lb chestnuts
200 g/7 oz granulated
sugar
150 g/5 oz baking
chocolate, grated
1 tbsp rum
70 g/2½ oz icing sugar

With a sharp, pointed knife cut an X on the flat side of each chestnut. Place them in cold water. Bring to the boil and cook for 25 minutes. Peel and mash them, then place in a saucepan with the granulated sugar and 3 tablespoons water. Stir constantly. When the sugar has dissolved remove from the heat and stir in the grated chocolate and the rum. Leave to cool slightly, then shape into little balls. Roll in the icing sugar or cocoa powder and chill in the refrigerator for 3 to 4 hours before serving.

Chilled orange soufflé

3 oranges
2 tbsp Grand Marnier
3 egg yolks
125 g/4 oz sugar
2 tbsp Cointreau
200 g/7 oz whipped cream
1 tbsp icing sugar

Carefully remove the rind, but not the pith, from one orange. Cut the rind into narrow strips, then cut the strips into small pieces, and blanch for 2 minutes. Cool under running water, then leave to stand for 2 hours in the Grand Marnier. Beat the egg yolks until creamy, place half the sugar and 50 ml/2 fl oz water in a saucepan and heat until the sugar dissolves. Do not allow to boil. Pour the sugar syrup in a thin stream into the beaten egg yolks. Stir in the Cointreau, the orange rind, and the juice of half an orange

and continue to beat for 3 minutes. Fold in the whipped cream. Chill 4 individual moulds in the freezer for 15 minutes. Pour the mixture into the moulds and place in the freezer for 4 hours. Carefully peel the rind, but not the pith, from another orange and blanch for 2 minutes. Place in a saucepan with the remaining sugar, the juice of 2 oranges, and 125 ml/4 fl oz water. Simmer for 5 minutes, skim the surface, and leave to stand for 30 minutes. Pour through a sieve and then into 4 serving dishes. Dip the soufflé moulds into hot water for a few seconds, then turn into the orange sauce. Sprinkle with icing sugar.

Flambéed apricots

40 g/1½ oz butter
4 strips lemon rind, cut
lengthwise
4 tbsp sugar
20 tinned apricot halves
225 ml/8 fl oz Cognac

Melt the butter in a large non-stick frying pan. Add the lemon rind and fry briefly. Dissolve the sugar in 4 tablespoons water and add to the frying pan with the drained apricots. Heat gently for 5 minutes, pour in the Cognac; when the sauce has thickened slightly, flame and serve immediately.

Flambéed pineapple

40 g/1½ oz butter
4 tinned pineapple rings
4 tbsp sugar
4 large strawberries
225 ml/8 fl oz rum

Melt the butter. Add the drained pineapple and the sugar, dissolved in few tablespoons of water. Heat gently for 3 to 4 minutes, then add the whole strawberries and the rum. When the sauce has thickened slightly place a strawberry in the centre of each pineapple ring and flame.

Floating islands

300 ml/10 fl oz milk
small piece vanilla
4 eggs
225 g/8 oz sugar
2 tbsp toasted slivered almonds

Bring the milk and the vanilla to the boil. Beat the egg yolks with 125 g/4 oz sugar in a saucepan. Add the cooled vanilla-flavoured milk, stirring constantly. Pour through a sieve, discard the vanilla and stir for 3 minutes over moderate heat until the custard thickens. Pour into individual dishes or glasses and leave to chill in the refrigerator. In a large saucepan heat 300 ml/10 fl oz water to a fairly high temperature. Whisk 2 egg whites until stiff, working in 50 g/2 oz sugar. Whisk for 1 minute. Spoon the meringue in 4 mounds into the saucepan and poach for 3 minutes. Turn them with a slotted spoon and cook for a further 3 minutes. Drain for 5 minutes on kitchen paper, then spoon the meringues on top of the chilled custard. Sprinkle with toasted almonds. Heat 50 g/2 oz sugar and 2 to 3 tablespoons water in a saucepan until it begins to caramelize. Leave to cool slightly, then pour over the meringues.

Fruit salad in gin

1 apple
1 banana
125 g/4 oz strawberries
10 cherries
1 peach
150 ml/5 fl oz gin
1 lemon
2 tbsp sugar

Peel the fruit and cut into pieces or slices. Mix together the gin, lemon juice, and sugar and pour over the fruit salad.

Hazelnut ice cream log

4 egg yolks
125 g/4 oz sugar
250 ml/9 fl oz milk
50 g/2 oz ground hazelnuts
125 ml/4 fl oz whipped cream

Place an ice cream mould in the freezer. Beat 2½ egg yolks with 25 g/1 oz sugar for 2 minutes. Bring the milk to the boil. In a separate saucepan heat 50 g/2 oz sugar and 125 ml/4 fl oz water until the sugar caramelizes. Dip the bottom of the saucepan in hot water for a few seconds, then pour the caramel in a thin stream into the milk, stirring vigorously. Add the beaten egg yolks and heat for 3 minutes, stirring constantly; do not allow to boil. Pour through a sieve into a basin and leave to cool, stirring occasionally. Pour into the cooled ice cream mould, level the surface, and place in the freezer. Beat 1½ egg yolks with a whisk. Place 25 g/1 oz sugar and 50 ml/2 fl oz water in a saucepan and heat to a fairly high temperature. Pour the syrup in a thin stream into the egg yolks and stir vigorously for 5 minutes. Add the ground hazelnuts and continue to beat until the mixture has cooled. Fold in the whipped cream. Pour on top of the ice cream, cover with waxed paper, and return to the freezer for 3 hours. Dip the mould in hot water for a few seconds and turn out on to a well chilled serving dish.

Ladies' kisses

125 g/4 oz plain flour
25 g/1 oz ground almonds
25 g/1 oz ground hazelnuts
50 g/2 oz sugar
pinch salt
few drops vanilla essence
50 g/2 oz butter
70 g/2½ oz baking chocolate

Work the flour, ground nuts, sugar, salt, and vanilla essence into the softened butter. Form into a ball and place for 1 hour

in the refrigerator. Break off pieces of the dough, roll into small balls, and place on a buttered baking tray. Press down lightly to flatten. Bake for 15 minutes in a preheated oven at 180°C/350°F/mark 4. Leave to cool. Melt the chocolate in a basin over simmering water and use to sandwich the halves together.

Lemon soufflé

50 g/2 oz butter
150 g/5 oz sugar
50 g/2 oz plain flour
3 eggs
3 egg yolks
3 lemons
400 ml/14 fl oz milk

Butter 4 individual soufflé dishes and sprinkle with sugar. Place the flour and 50 g/2 oz sugar in a saucepan with 1 whole egg, 1 egg yolk, and the juice of one lemon and whisk for 1 minute over low heat. Add the rind of one lemon to half the milk and bring to the boil. Add to the egg mixture and stir over moderate heat for 2 minutes. Remove from the heat. Add another egg yolk and the butter and beat well for 1 minute. Whisk 2 egg whites until stiff and fold into the mixture. Pour into the soufflé dishes and fill to within 5 mm/¼ in of the top. Place in a preheated oven at 190°C/375°F/mark 5 for 20 minutes. Beat the remaining egg yolks and sugar in a saucepan. Bring the remaining milk to the boil, cool and stir into the egg and sugar mixture. Cook gently until just before it reaches boiling point; remove from the heat and sieve. Add the juice of 2 lemons and stir well. Pour the hot sauce into heated individual dishes and unmould the soufflés into the centre.

Lemon tart

250 g/9 oz plain flour
salt
250 g/9 oz butter
125 g/4 oz sugar
3 eggs

4 tbsp milk
2 lemons
2 tbsp icing sugar

Make the pastry: sift the flour with a pinch of salt. Cut or rub in 200 g/7 oz butter and 50 g/2 oz sugar. Beat 1 egg with the milk and stir into the flour. Knead lightly to obtain a smooth dough. Wrap in waxed paper and chill in the refrigerator for 4 hours. Roll out the pastry to 3 mm/⅛ in and line a 30-cm/12-in floured and buttered flan tin. With the remaining pastry roll out a strip and press around the edges of the tin. Prick the pastry to prevent it rising and bake blind for 15 minutes at 130°C/250°F/mark ½ . Allow to cool. Beat 2 egg yolks in a basin with 50 g/2 oz sugar for about 1 minute. Place the basin over a saucepan of hot water and stir until the mixture thickens. Add 50 g/2 oz butter in pieces and heat gently for a further 3 minutes. Add the juice of 2 lemons and stir for 5 minutes. The lemon cream should be fairly liquid. Remove from the heat. Whisk the egg whites with a pinch of salt and fold gently into the lemon cream. Pour into the flan tin and sprinkle with icing sugar. Place in the oven at 240°C/475°F/mark 9 for 3 minutes. Leave to cool. Before serving decorate with a few slices of lemon.

Passion fruit sorbet

350 g/12 oz sugar
250 ml/9 fl oz water
1 kg/2¼ lb passion fruit

Place the sugar and water in a saucepan over high heat. Stir until the sugar has dissolved. Bring to the boil and leave to cool. Cut the passion fruit in half, discard the seeds, and scoop out the flesh. Liquidize briefly in a blender or food processor. Add to the sugar syrup and pour into a container. Mix well. Chill in the freezer for at least 1 hour. Serve in chilled individual dishes.

Peach and Moscato cream with zabaglione

800 g/1¾ lb firm peaches
250 g/9 oz sugar
250 ml/9 fl oz Moscato
6 eggs
knob of butter

Peel and pit the peaches and place in a saucepan with the sugar and Moscato. Cook until the liquid has evaporated. Sieve the cooked peaches and stir in the eggs, one at a time. Butter an ovenproof dish and pour in the peach mixture. Place the dish in a roasting tin half filled with hot water and bake for 20 minutes at 180°C/350°F/mark 4. Serve warm or chilled with Moscato flavoured zabaglione.

Pear flan

Puff pastry (page 181)
400 g/14 oz pears
125 g/4 oz sugar
500 ml/18 fl oz water
½ lemon

Prepare the pastry. Peel the pears, cut into quarters, and remove the core. Place in a saucepan with the sugar and grated rind of half a lemon. Cover with water and cook for 15 minutes. Drain and leave to cool. Roll out the pastry to a 3-mm/⅛-in thick circle and use to line a buttered flan tin. Prick the surface with a fork. Slice the pears finely and place, slightly overlapping, on top. Bake in a preheated oven at 230°C/450°F/mark 8 for 20 minutes.

Pineapple Bavarian cream with puréed strawberries

6 egg yolks
350 g/12 oz sugar
500 ml/18 fl oz milk
2 level tbsp powdered gelatine
250 ml/9 fl oz double cream
1 tsp vanilla sugar
4 slices pineapple
450 g/1 lb strawberries
4 large whole strawberries

Beat the egg yolks with 200 g/7 oz sugar. Stir in the hot milk and heat gently for a few minutes, stirring constantly until the custard thickens. Dissolve the gelatine in 125 ml/4 fl oz water in a basin over a pan of hot water. Stir into the custard and leave to cool slightly. Whip the cream and vanilla sugar (not too stiffly) and fold carefully into the cooled custard. Heat the pineapple slices for 10 minutes in 25 g/1 oz sugar until all the liquid is absorbed. Place a slice in each of 4 moulds and fill with the custard. Chill in the refrigerator for a few hours. Place the strawberries and remaining sugar in a blender and blend for 2 minutes. Strain through a fine sieve. Unmould the pineapple Bavarian cream on to individual dishes and serve with the strawberry purée. Decorate with the whole strawberries.

Pineapple ice cream

1 1-kg/2¼-lb pineapple
250 g/9 oz sugar
50 ml/2 fl oz water
3 eggs
200 ml/7 fl oz whipped cream
1 orange
1 tbsp icing sugar

Cut the pineapple in half lengthwise, leaving the leaves attached; scoop out the flesh, discarding the hard central core, and chill the empty containers in the refrigerator for 2 hours. Liquidize the flesh briefly in a blender or food processor. Place in a saucepan with 150 g/5 oz sugar and heat gently for 15 minutes until slightly reduced. Leave to cool. Place 50 g/2 oz sugar in another saucepan with the water and heat quickly. Beat the 3 egg yolks and stir in the sugar solution, beating hard to avoid lumps. Beat for 3 minutes. Stir in the puréed pineapple, then carefully fold in the whipped cream. Pour the mixture into the chilled half pineapple and place in the freezer for 3 hours. Whisk the egg whites with 50 g/2 oz sugar. Add the grated orange rind and spoon into a piping bag. Just before serving pipe the meringue around the pineapple, sprinkle with icing sugar and brown under a hot grill. Serve at once.

Raspberry Bavarian cream

500 g/1 lb 2 oz raspberries
juice of 1 lemon
6 egg yolks
225 g/8 oz sugar
2 level tbsp powdered gelatine
125 ml/4 fl oz double cream
75 ml/3 fl oz whipped cream

Liquidize the raspberries, reserving several whole ones for decoration, with the lemon juice and 40 g/1½ oz sugar. Pour through a nylon sieve. Beat the egg yolks with 150 g/5 oz sugar, then mix with the raspberry purée. Heat gently, stirring constantly, until the mixture thickens. Remove from the heat. Dissolve the gelatine in 125 ml/4 fl oz water in a basin over a pan of hot water. Stir into the raspberry mixture and leave to cool. Whip the double cream not too stiffly, with 40 g/1½ oz sugar and fold carefully into the raspberry custard; chill in the refrigerator for a few hours. To unmould, dip briefly in hot water. Invert on to a serving dish and decorate with the whipped cream and the whole raspberries.

Raspberries with zabaglione

4 egg yolks
175 g/6 oz sugar
125 ml/4 fl oz water
2 tbsp raspberry liqueur or Kirsch
700 g/1½ lb raspberries

Place the egg yolks in a deep basin with 125 g/4 oz sugar and the water over a pan of gently simmering water. Whisk continuously until the mixture becomes thick and creamy. Add the liqueur at the very end. Liquidize half the raspberries with 50 g/2 oz sugar. Spoon the whole raspberries into individual dishes and pour over the zabaglione. Place under a hot grill for a few minutes before pouring over the warmed raspberry purée.

Rhubarb soufflé

150 g/5 oz rhubarb, trimmed
80 g/3 oz icing sugar
150 g/5 oz granulated sugar
200 ml/7 fl oz water
3 eggs, separated
200 ml/7 fl oz milk

Cut the rhubarb into 2-cm/¾-in pieces. Place in a bowl, cover with the icing sugar and leave for 2 hours. Butter 4 individual soufflé dishes and sprinkle with sugar. Reserve 25 g/1 oz rhubarb and liquidize the rest. Bring 50 g/2 oz sugar and the water to the boil; add the purée and reserved pieces of rhubarb and cook for 2 minutes. Whisk 3 egg whites until stiff, add the rhubarb mixture, and whisk for another minute. Pour into the soufflé dishes. Place in a preheated oven at 170°C/325°F/mark 3 for 20 minutes. In a clean saucepan beat 3 egg yolks with the remaining sugar; add the milk and bring to the boil. Pour the sauce into heated individual dishes and unmould the soufflés into the centre.

Sablés

200 g/7 oz butter
150 g/5 oz icing sugar
3 eggs
40 g/1½ oz ground almonds
250 g/9 oz plain flour
grated rind of ½ lemon or orange
pinch salt

Cream the butter with half the sugar. Beat in 2 eggs and the remaining sugar, the ground almonds, flour, grated lemon or orange rind, and salt. Knead lightly and shape into a ball. Wrap in a clean cloth and chill in the refrigerator for a few hours. Roll out the dough to 5 mm/¼ in thick and cut out shapes with cutters dipped in flour. Place on a buttered baking tray, brush with egg, and bake for 15 to 20 minutes at 180°C/350°F/mark 4. Place the biscuits on a rack and leave to cool.

Strawberries and bananas au citron

2 bananas
200 g/7 oz strawberries
2 tbsp sugar
½ lemon

Slice the bananas and cut the strawberries in half. Dissolve the sugar in the lemon juice and pour over the fruit.

Strawberries in Champagne

450 g/1 lb strawberries
4 tsp Kirsch
4 tbsp sugar
500 ml/18 fl oz Champagne

Hull the strawberries and rinse in cold water. Dry thoroughly with kitchen paper. Spoon the strawberries into 4 individual dishes, heaping them into a mound. Sprinkle with a little Kirsch and then with sugar. Chill in the refrigerator. Pour the Champagne over the strawberries just before serving.

Wild strawberries and ice cream

400 g/14 oz strawberries
3 tbsp sugar
4 scoops vanilla ice cream
150 ml/5 fl oz whipping cream
1 tsp Kirsch
4 candied violets

Rinse the strawberries in cold water and dry thoroughly. Sprinkle with 2 tablespoons sugar and place in 4 individual dishes. Sprinkle with a little more sugar and place a scoop of ice cream in each dish. Whip the cream until stiff and spoon over the ice cream. Before serving sprinkle with a few drops of Kirsch and decorate with a candied violet.

Zabaglione

6 egg yolks
4 tbsp sugar
150 ml/5 fl oz Marsala
16 langues de chat or sponge fingers

In a basin or double saucepan beat together the egg yolks and sugar, gradually adding the Marsala. Heat gently over a saucepan of simmering water, beating with a balloon whisk or electric mixer, until thick and creamy. Serve at once in individual glass dishes with *langues de chat* or sponge fingers.

Basic preparations

Beurre blanc

1 large shallot, chopped
2 tbsp white wine vinegar
1½ tbsp white wine
1½ tbsp fumet (see below)
125 g/4 oz butter
salt
pepper

Place the shallot, vinegar, wine, and fumet in a saucepan and cook over moderate heat until the liquid has reduced by three-quarters. Remove from the heat. Leave to cool slightly before beating in the butter as quickly as possible, one piece at a time. Make sure the butter is well blended and the sauce pale and creamy. Season with salt and pepper. (If the sauce turns transparent, plunge the bottom of the saucepan into ice cold water until the sauce thickens.)

Clarified butter

450 g/1 lb butter

Melt the butter in a saucepan over moderate heat and simmer for 5 minutes. Remove any surface scum with a slotted spoon, then pour the ghee (clarified butter) into a clean basin, making sure the residue which collects in the bottom of the saucepan is left behind.

Court-bouillon (for 1 kg/2¼ lb fish)

1 carrot
5 peppercorns
2 litres/3½ pints water
125 ml/4 fl oz white wine
50 ml/2 fl oz white wine
  vinegar
½ tbsp sea salt
½ stick celery
2 sprigs parsley
½ onion
½ bay leaf
pinch thyme

Cut the carrot into four lengthwise, crush the peppercorns, and place all the ingredients in a large saucepan. Bring to the boil, simmer for 30 minutes, then strain through a sieve. This rich *court-bouillon* is ideal for fish such as turbot and eel. For a simpler version, reduce the quantity of vegetables and use half the quantity of wine and vinegar.

Fumet de poisson

25 g/1 oz butter
½ onion
450 g/1 lb fish trimmings,
  heads, bones, etc.
½ stick celery
white part of 1 leek
5 crushed peppercorns
125 ml/4 fl oz white wine
1 litre/1¾ pints water
bouquet garni (2 sprigs
  parsley, sprig thyme, ½
  bay leaf)

Melt the butter in a large saucepan and brown the sliced onion. Add the fish trimmings and all remaining ingredients except the water and stir for a few minutes. Add the water, bring to the boil, and simmer, covered, for 30 minutes, skimming the surface occasionally with a slotted spoon. Leave to cool, strain, and reduce by boiling over moderate heat for a few minutes.

Lemon marinade

2–3 lemons

Lemons are used as a marinade for raw fish. Clean, rinse, and dry the fish and leave to stand in the lemon juice for 30 minutes to 1 hour, depending on the size of the fish. Do not leave for too long as the acid will make the flesh flaccid.

Puff pastry

450 g/1 lb plain flour
½ tsp salt
225 ml/8 fl oz water
450 g/1 lb butter

Sift the flour and salt into a large bowl. Rub in a knob of the butter, add the water gradually and mix to form a smooth dough. Wrap in a clean cloth and place in the refrigerator for 30 minutes. Shape the butter into a rectangle. Roll out the dough into a square. Place the butter in the middle and fold over the edges of the dough to enclose it. Sprinkle lightly with flour and roll out into a 1-cm/½-in thick rectangle. Fold into three, folding the bottom third up and the top third down. Roll out into a rectangle the same size as before. Make a quarter turn and fold the dough in three again. Wrap in waxed paper and place in the refrigerator for 1 hour. Repeat the rolling out and folding operations twice more. Place the dough in the refrigerator for another hour. Remove 1 hour before the dough is required.

Vinegar marinade

onions
wine vinegar
peppercorns
bay leaf

Peel and slice the onions and place all the ingredients in a shallow dish. Leave the fish in the marinade for 1 to 3 days. (The onions may be browned slightly first.) A vinegar marinade is often used for fried fish to give a more pronounced flavour. It can also be used as a means of preserving fish for several days.

Sauces

The following selection includes some of the most traditional sauces which may be served as an accompaniment to a variety of fish dishes.

Aïoli

4 cloves garlic
2 egg yolks
salt and pepper
250 ml/9 fl oz olive oil
1 lemon

Peel the garlic and crush in a mortar. Stir together the egg yolks, garlic, and salt and pepper. Pour in the oil a drop at a time, stirring constantly. Add the lemon juice in the same way and continue stirring until smooth.

Anchovy mayonnaise

mayonnaise made with 2 egg yolks (see recipe)
4 anchovy fillets
1 tbsp lemon juice

Finely chop the anchovies, mix with the lemon juice, and stir into the mayonnaise until well blended.

Béarnaise sauce

Makes approximately 250 ml/9 fl oz
2 shallots
125 ml/4 fl oz white wine
4 tbsp vinegar
1½ tbsp chopped tarragon
1½ tbsp chopped chervil
3 egg yolks
250 g/9 oz butter
salt
pinch Cayenne pepper

Finely chop the shallots and place in a saucepan with the wine, vinegar, and 1 tablespoon each tarragon and chervil. Reduce over low heat for about 15 minutes until approximately 4 tablespoons of liquid remain. Strain through a chinois, pressing well to extract as much liquid as possible. Pour into a double saucepan or into a small basin over a saucepan of simmering water. Mix in the egg yolks, beating with a whisk. Gradually add the softened butter, beating carefully and making sure that each piece is well blended before adding the next. Remove from the heat and continue beating. The sauce should be quite thick. Add the remaining tarragon and chervil and season with salt and Cayenne pepper. Mix well.

Dill sauce
See page 121.

Green mayonnaise

mayonnaise made with 2 egg yolks (see recipe above right)
50 g/2 oz spinach
a few basil leaves
small bunch parsley
salt and pepper

Wash the spinach leaves thoroughly in cold running water to remove all traces of grit. Cook briefly in a covered saucepan with no added water. Drain when tender and chop finely. Chop the basil and parsley and mix with the spinach. Work into the mayonnaise and season with salt and pepper.

Hollandaise sauce

2 large egg yolks
1 tbsp white wine vinegar
salt
pepper
200 g/7 oz butter
1 tbsp lemon juice

Beat together in a small basin or double saucepan the egg yolks, vinegar, and salt and pepper. Heat very gently over a saucepan of gently simmering water, stirring constantly and adding the butter one piece at a time. Make sure each piece is well blended before adding the next. When all the butter is added and the sauce coats the back of a spoon, remove from the heat and stir in the lemon juice. Mix well and serve hot.

Mayonnaise

2 egg yolks
salt and pepper
250 ml/9 fl oz olive oil
1 tbsp lemon juice

Beat the egg yolks with salt and pepper until they thicken slightly. Gradually add the oil, a drop at a time to begin with, beating constantly, until the sauce is smooth and well blended. Add the lemon juice last of all.

Nantua sauce

250 g/9 oz freshwater crayfish
salt
150 g/5 oz butter
25 g/1 oz plain flour
250 ml/9 fl oz milk
250 ml/9 fl oz fumet (page 181)
pepper
250 ml/9fl oz double cream

Boil the crayfish whole in salted water for 8 minutes without peeling; chop into pieces while still hot. Place in a blender with 125 g/4 oz melted butter and liquidize. Strain through a fine sieve. Make a white sauce: melt the remaining butter in a saucepan. Stir in the flour and cook gently for 2 minutes. Remove from the heat and stir in a little hot milk. Beat until smooth. Return to the heat and add the remaining milk and fumet. Season with salt and pepper. Bring to the boil, them simmer for 3 minutes. Add the cream and reduce slightly. Remove from the heat and stir in the crayfish butter.

Polish sauce
See page 147.

Rémoulade sauce

400 ml/14 fl oz mayonnaise
1 tsp mustard
1 tsp capers
1 tsp gherkins
½ tsp chopped basil
½ tsp chopped parsley
1 tsp anchovy paste

Mix together the mayonnaise and mustard. Stir well and add the chopped capers, gherkins, basil, and parsley. When these ingredients are well blended, stir in the anchovy paste and mix well.

Sauce Louis
See page 104.

Scampi sauce
See page 82.

'Tarator' sauce
See page 46.

Tartare sauce

2 hard-boiled egg yolks
400 ml/14 fl oz oil
salt and pepper
1 tbsp finely chopped chives
1 tbsp mayonnaise
1 tsp vinegar

Finely sieve the egg yolks. Add the oil in a thin stream, stirring constantly. Season with salt and pepper. Add the chives, mayonnaise, and vinegar and stir well until the sauce is smooth.

Tuna mayonnaise

80 g/3 oz tinned tuna
6 anchovy fillets
2 hard-boiled eggs
250 ml/9 fl oz olive oil
juice of ½ lemon
1 tbsp chopped parsley
salt and pepper

Pound the tuna and anchovy fillets. Mash the egg yolks with a fork and mix with the tuna and anchovy paste. Gradually work in the oil and lemon juice. Add the chopped parsley and season with salt and pepper.

Choosing, cooking and storing fish

Choosing fish

For serious cooks and lovers of fish, truly fresh fish can only be considered that which is sorted into shallow boxes on a bed of ice and transported immediately to a quayside market as soon as it is caught. When buying fish it is essential to know how to judge its freshness from its appearance, texture, and smell.

Freshly caught fish is quite stiff, although this characteristic changes after only a few hours; the skin is taut, bright, and shiny; the scales lie flat against the body, which is covered with a thin, translucent film. The pupil should be dark and bright and the cornea shining and transparent. The flesh beneath the gill flap should be bright red and the fish should be firm and resistant to the touch; the flesh should spring back when pressed lightly, leaving no impression.

As for judging the freshness of fish by its smell, a few simple comparisons may help: fresh fish should smell of the sea and of the strong but pleasant saltiness of seaweed. When checking the freshness of molluscs and crustaceans the appearance of the body is the most important indicator; crustaceans should be shiny, wet, firm, and vividly coloured with their legs or claws firmly attached to their bodies. They should smell fresh and of the sea. The colour of the body of molluscs may vary, depending on their colour when caught, as they often camouflage themselves. The whiteness of the flesh of cuttlefish and squid is a sign of freshness; yellow or brownish patches show that they are too old. The state of the shells is a good indication of the freshness of mussels, clams, or oysters. They should be tightly closed or should snap shut when sharply tapped if the molluscs are still alive. As with fish, they should smell pleasantly salty.

Cooking fish

Fish lends itself to all kinds of methods of cooking, depending on the quality and texture of the flesh: it can be poached, cooked in foil (*en papillote*), shallow fried, deep fried, baked, grilled, barbecued, braised, or steamed.

Poaching
The fish is simmered in a rich vegetable *court-bouillon* or lighter stock (see page 181), depending on the type of fish. The stock should be allowed to cool before use and should always be kept below boiling point while the fish is cooking.

Cooking in foil
Fish cooked *en papillote* is placed together with the herbs and seasonings in the centre of a well buttered sheet of foil. The edges are folded tightly to seal, forming a loose parcel, and the fish is baked in the oven or cooked in a steamer.

Shallow frying
Suitable for fillets and steaks. The fish is usually dipped in flour then fried in melted butter or oil.

Deep frying
Suitable for whole fish or fillets coated in batter. The fish is cooked in hot oil (180°–190°C / 350–375°F) and should be drained on kitchen paper to absorb excess fat before serving.

Baking
All the ingredients, including the fish, are placed in an ovenproof dish or casserole and baked in the oven.

Grilling or barbecueing
The most important points to remember when cooking fish this way are the evenness of temperature and the distance of the fish from the source of heat. The fish should be cooked slowly and evenly. To prepare the fish, either soak in brine or brush with oil. Brush several times during cooking.

Braising
In this method the fish is browned lightly first in a little melted butter and then cooked either in the oven or on top of the stove in wine, stock, tomato sauce, or other liquid.

Steaming
The fish is cooked with herbs and seasonings on a plate or wrapped in foil, and placed in a perforated metal basket or steamer over a saucepan of simmering water.

Storing fish

To keep fish for a short period—not more than 24 hours—clean in the usual way and place in the refrigerator. To keep fish for longer than a day it should be stored in the freezer. Rinse and clean the fish thoroughly, dry with kitchen paper and cut into fillets or steaks. Wrap in polythene before freezing. Frozen fish, which strictly speaking should have been brought from room temperature to −18°C/0°F in less than 4 hours, should be stored at that temperature until it is used. Frozen fish is usually packaged in plastic bags so that you can check the state of the fish. Once removed from the freezer it must be used. Always pay careful attention to the recommended storage dates on frozen fish.

Equipment and utensils for preparing and cooking fish

1 Turbot kettle
2 Small saucepan
3 Round frying pan
4 Tall cooking pot
5 Straight-sided frying pan (skillet)
6 Small fish kettle
7 Skimmer
8 Balloon whisk
9 Double-sided fish mould
10 Chinois (fine strainer)

11 Cast-iron oval frying
    pan
12 Top of double
    saucepan
13 Wooden palette
14 Fish slice
15 Large fish kettle
16, 17 Ovenproof baking
    dishes
18 Fish scaler
19 Ladle
20 Double-ended scoop

21 Lobster crackers
22 Lemon zester
23 Filleting knife
24 Stainless steel scissors
25 Basting brush
26 Ramekins
27 Mesh ladle for deep
    frying
28 Sauce spoon
29 Wooden spoon
30 Small ladle
31 Chopping board

32 Vegetable chopper
33 Oyster knife
34 Large filleting knife
35 Paring knife
36 Chef's knife
37 Large sieve for
    coating with flour
38 Small ring moulds
39 Medium saucepan
40 Fish fork
41 Fish knife

How to clean fish, crustaceans and molluscs

Before cooking fish all the inedible parts should be removed: these include fins, scales, bones, head (optional), and entrails.

Fish

Scaling fish. Place the fish on a sheet of paper and, holding firmly by the tail, scrape off the scales with a blunt knife or a special fish scaler, working repeatedly from tail to head.

Gutting fish. This is perhaps the most important part of cleaning a fish and involves removing the entrails and rinsing the cavity. This operation should be carried out as soon as possible after the fish is bought.

Round fish For large fish, such as sea bass or mackerel, use a sharp knife or scissors to slit along the belly from the rear fin to just below the head (1). Open up and pull out the entrails (2). For small round fish, such as sardines or fresh anchovies, break off the head and squeeze the body slightly (3); the entrails should pull away quite easily.

Flat fish For flat fish, such as plaice, sole, and turbot, make a semi-circular cut behind the gills on the darker side (4). Squeeze out the entrails and rinse thoroughly. Cut away the fins using sharp scissors (5).

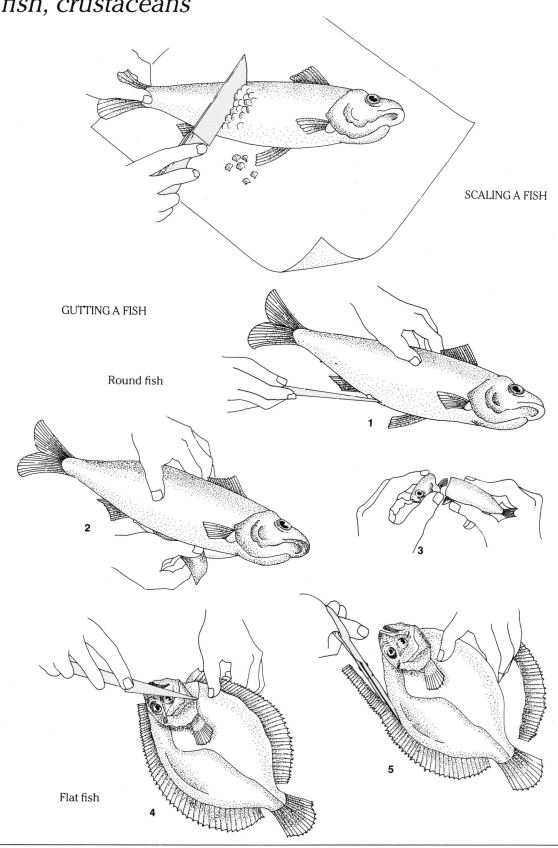

SCALING A FISH

GUTTING A FISH

Round fish

Flat fish

186

Skinning fish. To skin a particularly difficult fish such as an eel, suspend the eel from a hook or door handle on a piece of strong rope and make a cut right around the eel just below the gills (1). Peel back enough skin to give you a firm grip (2). Rub the skin and your hands with salt for a firmer hold and then pull the skin down towards the tail (3).

Eel

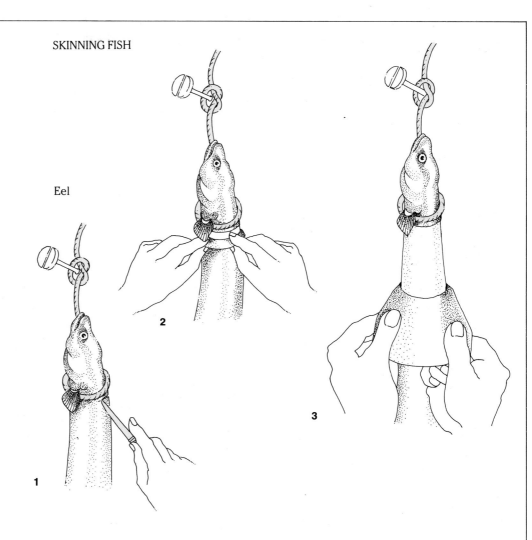

Flat fish Usually only the dark skin is removed from flat fish. Make a cut just above the tail (4), then, holding the fish firmly, peel the skin gently towards the head (5).

Flat fish

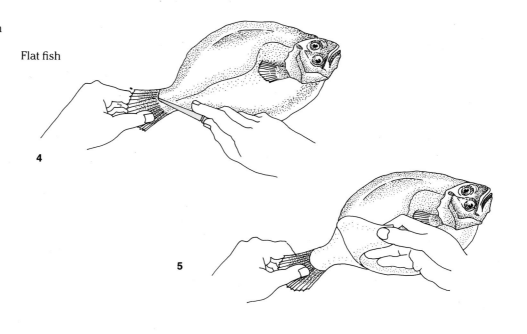

Filleting fish. For this job an extremely sharp knife with a thin blade is essential.

Round fish Cut right along the backbone (1) then carefully cut away the upper fillet in one piece, holding the knife close against the bones and working from head to tail (2). Turn the fish over and repeat the operation.

Flat fish Cut down the centre of the fish from head to tail (3); holding the knife close to the bones, cut away the fillets one side at a time (4). Turn the fish over and repeat the operation.

Crustaceans

Lobsters. After boiling the lobster, break off the head (1); place the tail on a board and cut lengthwise through the shell (2); prise open carefully and remove the flesh (3).

Prawns. Pull away the head from the tail (1); then remove the meat carefully from the tail section (2), discarding the central black vein (the intestine).

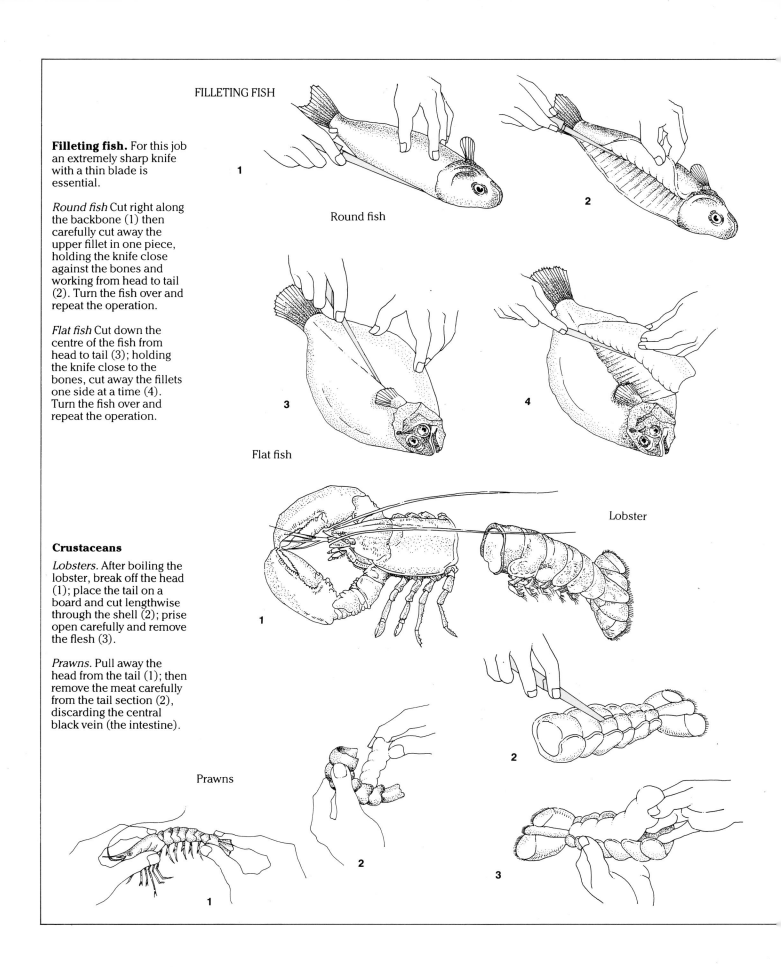

Round fish

Flat fish

Lobster

Prawns

Molluscs

To clean an *octopus* lift up the large sac-like part and turn completely inside out (1); discard the entrails, then with a sharp knife cut away the eyes and the beak in the centre of the tentacles (2).

To clean *cuttlefish* and *squid* pull the head and tentacles away from the body (1), discarding the entrails and ink sac; remove the hard transparent bone by pressing in the bottom of the body sac (2).

Mussels and clams should be rinsed for at least 1 hour, preferably under running water, to remove all traces of sand. Scrub mussels with a stiff brush (2) and trim away the beard (3).

When cooking mussels or clams heat gently as directed until the shells open. Discard any which do not.

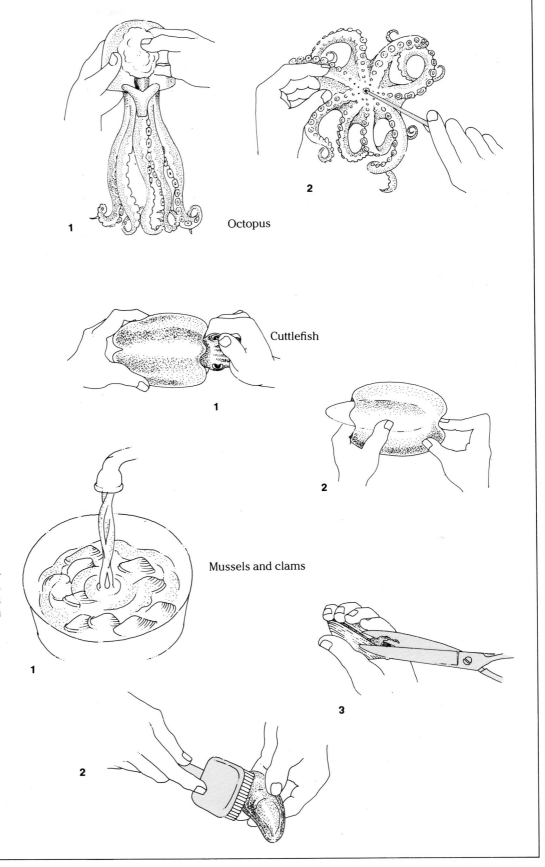

Octopus

Cuttlefish

Mussels and clams

Index